CRITICAL THINKING
BOOK 1

by
Anita Harnadek

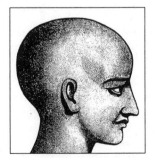

© 1981
CRITICAL THINKING PRESS & SOFTWARE
(formerly Midwest Publications)
P.O. Box 448 • Pacific Grove • CA 93950-0448
Phone 800-458-4849 • FAX 408-372-3230
ISBN 0-910974-75-6
Printed in the United States of America

ACKNOWLEDGMENTS

The following people and organizations have my sincere appreciation for their helpful information and suggestions for material for this book: Joseph Rohrig; Delores Lobdell; Frank Sasso, Jr.; Ru-Mei and Lila Kung; Joy Tellefsen; Diane Heussner; Winona Shingler; police departments of St. Clair Shores, Michigan and Sault Ste. Marie, Michigan; the public library and the public elementary school on Drummond Island, Michigan.

Also, many ideas for material for this book came from various advertisements and from newspaper and magazine articles, editorials, and letters to the editors.

TO THE STUDENT

Former students are often heard to say that school did not prepare them for the real world. They say that they had to learn things in school that they've never used after school. They say that they had to learn a lot of facts or figures or rules that don't matter in everyday life.

One of the most valuable things a school today can teach its students is how to think critically. Although every normal human being does some thinking, he isn't exactly a champion at <u>critical</u> thinking. Maybe that's one of the reasons the world is in such a mess today.

Thinking critically is a skill, just as skating, driving, and carpentry are skills. And like any other skill, it can be taught, it can be learned, and it can improve with practice and daily use.

The purpose of this book is to get you started in developing the skill of thinking critically. How to develop your ability to think critically is one thing you'll learn in school which <u>will</u> be of use to you in the real world!

TO THE TEACHER

As mentioned above, skating, driving, and carpentry are skills. The student does not learn to do these things by sitting in a classroom and being told how to do them. Although he can be given classroom lessons in techniques, we know he must practice these techniques in order to acquire the skill.

We also know that when a student keeps getting wrong results, it is not enough to tell him how to get correct results — we must also show him what he is doing wrong and **why** his method **is** wrong.

Critical thinking is a skill which must be practiced in order to develop effectively. It follows that it is not enough to tell the student about techniques, then have him do exercises, and then simply tell him the "right" answers. He must also be given the chance to examine both his reasons for choosing his answers and the reasons other students chose their "right" answers. **This will not be done by using this textbook as a workbook.**

The most effective way to achieve the desired results is to center the course around **class discussion. The students will learn to think critically not only by expressing their opinions and hearing rebuttals from their classmates, but by listening to the discussions among their classmates.**

TABLE OF CONTENTS

CHAPTER 1 — INTRODUCTION TO CRITICAL THINKING

1.1 WHAT IS CRITICAL THINKING? 2
1.2 WHO CAN LEARN TO THINK CRITICALLY? 3
1.3 WHAT ARE YOU EXPECTED TO LEARN IN THIS
       CHAPTER? 4
1.4 DISCUSSIONS, DISAGREEMENTS, ARGUMENTS,
       AND FIGHTS 5
1.5 WHEN IS IT STUPID TO ARGUE? 7
1.6 GENERAL STATEMENTS 10
1.7 COUNTEREXAMPLES 12
1.8 "PROOF" BY FAILURE TO FIND A COUNTER-
       EXAMPLE 14
1.9 IS YOUR THINKING STUCK IN A RUT? 15
1.10 CHAPTER REVIEW PROBLEMS AND QUESTIONS 22

CHAPTER 2 — INTRODUCTION TO LOGIC

2.1 SYMBOLS USED IN THIS CHAPTER. 26
2.2 "OR" SENTENCES AND THEIR TRUTH VALUES 28
2.3 "AND" SENTENCES AND THEIR TRUTH VALUES 30
2.4 DOUBLE NEGATIVES AND MULTIPLE "∼" SIGNS 32
2.5 NECESSARY AND SUFFICIENT CONDITIONS 34
2.6 "IF-THEN" SENTENCES 36
2.7 TRUTH VALUES OF "IF-THEN" SENTENCES. 37
2.8 PROPOSITION, CONVERSE, INVERSE,
       CONTRAPOSITIVE 42
2.9 SUBSTITUTION OF CONVERSE OR INVERSE FOR
       ITS PROPOSITION 46
2.10 "ONLY IF" SENTENCES AND THEIR TRUTH VALUES 47
2.11 ARGUMENTS, PREMISES, AND CONCLUSIONS 50
2.12 CHAPTER REVIEW PROBLEMS AND QUESTIONS 53

CHAPTER 3 — SOME BASIC CONCEPTS FOR CRITICAL THINKING

3.1 WHAT'S THE DIFFERENCE BETWEEN "PROBABLE"
       AND "POSSIBLE"? 58
3.2 ALLEGORIES, OLD SAYINGS, AND LITERARY
       REFERENCES 59
3.3 PEOPLE MAY HAVE DIFFERENT FEELINGS ABOUT
       THE SAME WORD. 63
3.4 A CHANGED DEFINITION MAY PRODUCE A
       CHANGED CONCLUSION. 65
3.5 DON'T JUMP TO A CONCLUSION—THE OBVIOUS
       ONE MAY BE WRONG 70
3.6 EYEWITNESSES AND CIRCUMSTANTIAL EVIDENCE 72
3.7 IMPLICATIONS AND INFERENCES. 77
3.8 CHAPTER REVIEW PROBLEMS AND QUESTIONS 79

CHAPTER 4 — COMMON ERRORS IN REASONING

4.1 CIRCULAR REASONING. 86
4.2 "PROOF" BY SELECTED INSTANCES 87

4.3	AVOIDING THE QUESTION.	88
4.4	SPECIAL PLEADING	90
4.5	FAKING A CONNECTION	91
4.6	CHAPTER REVIEW PROBLEMS AND QUESTIONS.	93

CHAPTER 5 — PROPAGANDA TECHNIQUES

5.1	INTRODUCTION	98
5.2	"BANDWAGON"	99
5.3	REPETITION	100
5.4	"TRANSFER"	101
5.5	"TESTIMONIAL".	103
5.6	"EXIGENCY"	105
5.7	"FREE" AND "BARGAIN"	106
5.8	"GLITTERING GENERALITY"	108
5.9	INNUENDO	110
5.10	"NAME-CALLING"	112
5.11	MISCELLANEOUS TECHNIQUES.	114
5.12	CHAPTER REVIEW PROBLEMS AND QUESTIONS	116

CHAPTER 6 — ADVERTISING AND SCHEMES

6.1	INTRODUCTION.	120
6.2	"GET RICH QUICK" SCHEMES	120
6.3	WHAT'S IN A NAME?	122
6.4	ADVERTISING SELLS IDEAS	122
6.5	CAREER OPPORTUNITIES.	124
6.6	STUPID ADVERTISEMENTS	126
6.7	MISCELLANEOUS SCHEMES	127
6.8	ASKING QUESTIONS ABOUT ADVERTISEMENTS.	129
6.9	CHAPTER REVIEW PROBLEMS AND QUESTIONS	132

CHAPTER 7 — EXAMINING ARGUMENTS AND VALUE JUDGMENTS

7.1	RULES OF A SOCIETY	136
7.2	PROTECTION OF THE LAW	136
7.3	EMOTIONAL WORDS AND ARGUMENTS	140
7.4	DOUBLE STANDARDS	142
7.5	WHERE DO YOU DRAW THE LINE?	146
7.6	ATTRIBUTES OF A GOOD ARGUMENT	149
7.7	CHAPTER REVIEW PROBLEMS AND QUESTIONS	153

CHAPTER 8 — LEARNING TO BE OPEN-MINDED

8.1	INTRODUCTION.	156
8.2	LOOKING AT TWO SIDES OF AN ISSUE	157
8.3	RECOGNIZING ISSUES AND SUPPORTING POINTS	160
8.4	ANTICIPATING ARGUMENTS FOR THE OTHER SIDE	164
8.5	FINDING ARGUMENTS OF YOUR OWN.	166
8.6	DEBATING	167
8.7	CHAPTER REVIEW PROBLEMS AND QUESTIONS	170

GLOSSARY	173
INDEX	176

CHAPTER 1

INTRODUCTION TO CRITICAL THINKING

1.1   WHAT IS CRITICAL THINKING?

1.2   WHO CAN LEARN TO THINK CRITICALLY?

1.3   WHAT ARE YOU EXPECTED TO LEARN IN THIS CHAPTER?

1.4   DISCUSSIONS, DISAGREEMENTS, ARGUMENTS, AND FIGHTS

1.5   WHEN IS IT STUPID TO ARGUE?

1.6   GENERAL STATEMENTS

1.7   COUNTEREXAMPLES

1.8   ''PROOF'' BY FAILURE TO FIND A COUNTEREXAMPLE

1.9   IS YOUR THINKING STUCK IN A RUT?

1.10   CLASS DISCUSSION PROBLEMS AND QUESTIONS FOR CHAPTER REVIEW

1.1 WHAT IS CRITICAL THINKING?

Critical thinking is a term which includes many kinds of thinking all at once. When we say that someone is thinking critically, we do not mean that he is finding fault with something or that he is looking for a fight. We do mean all of the following:

1. He is open-minded about new ideas.
2. He does not argue about something when he knows nothing about it.
3. He knows when he needs more information about something.
4. He knows the difference between a conclusion which might be true and one which must be true.
5. He knows that people have different ideas about the meanings of words.
6. He tries to avoid common mistakes in his own reasoning.
7. He questions everything which doesn't make sense to him.
8. He tries to separate emotional thinking from logical thinking.
9. He tries to build up his vocabulary so that he can understand what other people are saying and so that he can make his own ideas clear to other people.

There are many other things a critical thinker does, but the list above is enough to give you a pretty good idea of some of the things we'll be working on in this book.

CLASS DISCUSSION PROBLEMS

For each problem, do two things:
(a) Tell whether or not John seems to be thinking critically.
(b) Tell why you think your answer is right.

Example:

Problem: Bill: "Do you think it's possible to build an airplane which would hold 10,000 passengers?"

John: "What a stupid question! It'd be too heavy to get off the ground. Man, where's your head, anyhow?!"

Answer: (a) No.

(b) First, John is not being open-minded about a new idea. (See item 1 on the list in this section.) Second, we might wonder if John knows enough about engineering to support his second sentence.
(See item 3 on the list in this section.)

Note: Your (b) answer could be shortened to this:
(b) See items 1 and 3 on the list.

1. John read a book which used a lot of words he didn't understand. He didn't bother to look up the words in a dictionary. John thought that the author must be pretty smart to use words like that, so he decided that the author must be right about what he said in the book.
2. John read in one book that all airplanes have only two wings, and he read in another book that some airplanes have four wings. John figured that nothing false would be printed in a book, so he thought that both statements were true.
3. John learned that some people connected with politics were sentenced to prison. He read the official records of the trials and decided that, based on these records, the sentences were fair.
4. Same as problem 3, and John also came to the conclusion that all people involved in politics deserve jail sentences.
5. Betty: "Transportation in the big cities is really a mess. Why don't the engineers come up with movable sidewalks so that people could go places without some kind of vehicle to carry them?"
   John: "Now that's really a dumb idea! I don't know anything about what kind of machinery it would take to do it, but I know it wouldn't work!"
6. Yoshia: "Dave is really a good student, isn't he? He gets nearly all A's."
   John: "Naw, he's not so good. He gets A's all right, but he studies like crazy."
7. Kathy: "How come you let Charlie get away with telling you that you acted like a 5-year-old? If anyone talked to me like that, I'd really tell him off!"
   John: "I wondered why he said that to me, so I asked him. I didn't agree with the reasons he gave, but I found out why he said it. I figured that made more sense than just yelling at him about it."

1.2 WHO CAN LEARN TO THINK CRITICALLY?

Here are some things you should know about critical thinking:
1. Almost everyone can learn to think critically.
2. The harder you try to think critically, the better you'll be at it.
3. You can learn to think better whether you're fast or slow at other things.
4. If you start being mixed up about ideas which you used to just accept or turn down, that's a good sign. It means that you're thinking about them instead of just saying, "OK, that's good," or, "No, I don't like that."

1.3 WHAT ARE YOU EXPECTED TO LEARN IN THIS CHAPTER?

You should already have learned some things in this chapter. From the first section, you should have learned about some of the things a critical thinker does. (At this point, you probably don't know exactly what each of the nine items listed in section 1.1 means, but your ideas will get clearer as you work through this book.) In the second section, you should have learned that you'll probably get better at thinking if you work at it, and you probably won't get better at thinking if you don't work at it.

What else should you learn in this chapter? It is hoped that you will learn all of these things:

1. Discussions, disagreements, arguments, fights, and temper tantrums are not all the same thing.

2. It is senseless to argue about a fact which is a matter of accurate public record.

3. There is a difference between a statement about all things and a statement about some things.

4. A counterexample is a certain kind of statement. It can be used to show someone that he's wrong.

4

5. A "proof" by failure to find a counterexample isn't really a proof at all.
6. Look at old ideas from fresh viewpoints.
7. There is a difference between a conclusion which <u>might</u> be true and a conclusion which <u>must</u> be true.

Keep the above goals in mind as you go through the rest of this chapter.

CLASS DISCUSSION PROBLEMS

This section lists seven things you're expected to learn in this chapter (besides what you've already learned). Each problem below states an idea. Tell whether each idea is true (T), false (F), or not listed (NL) to show whether or not the idea agrees with one of the seven listed. If your answer is "T" or "F" then give an item number to support your answer.

1. It's OK to argue about what Hank Aaron's batting average was during the regular season of 1973.
2. There's always a lot of angry yelling when two people in Diane's family disagree with each other, and it makes Diane nervous. There will be a lot of disagreements in this class, too. (Accept the first two statements as true.) So Diane must be nervous about being in this class.
3. If a conclusion might be true, then it must be true.
4. Suppose someone says he's going to tell you a new version of "Goldilocks and the Three Bears" and he says you're supposed to pretend you never heard any such story before. Suppose he also says he's going to ask you questions about the new story to see how closely you were listening. Then you should tell him not to bother, since it isn't possible to keep the old story separated from the new one in your mind.
5. Sometimes two words can mean the same thing if you look them up in the dictionary, but they can mean different things when different people use them.

1.4 DISCUSSIONS, DISAGREEMENTS, ARGUMENTS, AND FIGHTS

Just to make sure we all mean the same thing when we say, "discussion," "disagreement," "argument," or "fight," we'll define them in this section.

When we say that people are **discussing** something (or are having a **discussion**), we'll mean that they are talking about something. They may or may not agree with each other.

If we say that people **disagree** with each other (or are having a **disagreement**), we'll mean that each of them thinks the other person is wrong. You can doubt that the other person is right without thinking that he is wrong—that is, you can think that he may be wrong without thinking that he is wrong. In this case, you are neither agreeing nor disagreeing with him.

If we say that people are **arguing** (or are having an **argument**), we will mean that they disagree with each other and that each is trying to convince the other that he (the other person) is wrong. We will say that we don't have an argument until both people are arguing. That is, one person may tell the other that he's wrong (and so is arguing and may be trying to start an argument), but if the other person just accepts the comment, then we don't have an argument.[1]

If we say that two people are **fighting**—with words, of course—we will mean that they are arguing and have lost some control of themselves. (Maybe they are red in the faces or have lost control of their tempers or are shouting because they're angry.)

CLASS DISCUSSION PROBLEMS

Problems 1-10: Basing your answers on the definitions given in this section, tell whether each statement is true (T) or false (F).
1. Every fight is a disagreement.
2. Every disagreement is a fight.
3. Every fight is an argument.
4. Every argument is a fight.
5. Every disagreement is a discussion.
6. Every discussion is a disagreement.
7. If two people argue very long, they're bound to end up in a fight.
8. Every argument presupposes a disagreement. (That is, you can't have an argument without some kind of disagreement.)
9. It is possible for two people to agree on something and yet argue about it if one agrees to take the other side "just for the sake of argument."
10. Every disagreement results in an argument.

Problems 11-15: Tell whether each situation shows a discussion, a disagreement, an argument, or a fight. (It may be that some combination of these four things is at work—for example, maybe one person is arguing, and the other one is fighting.)
11. Mrs. Jones: "What do you think of Mrs. Johnson's new drapes?"

    Mrs. Nishiura: "I think they look nice. I'm glad she put something over those bare windows."

    Mrs. Jones: "She told me once that she liked the bare windows because it made her living room seem bigger."

---

[1] There is another kind of argument which we'll talk about in section 2.11. This other kind of argument involves a line of reasoning instead of a conversation.

12. Bob: "This is a good day for fishing. Let's go."
    Mark: "No, the wind isn't right."
13. (problem 12 continued) Bob: "Sure, it is. The wind is from the west, and you know the old saying, 'When the wind's from the west, then the fish bite the best!'"
14. (problem 13 continued) Mark: "Yeah, I forgot about that. OK, let's go."
15. Maureen: "Well, you sure took your time about getting here! You're over two hours late!"
    Dale: "I couldn't help it. I had to take my mother shopping first."
    Maureen: "Sure, you did. And I'll bet you had four flat tires and ran out of gas on the way, too!"
    Dale: "You don't have to be sarcastic about it! I got here as soon as I could and if that isn't good enough for you, that's tough rocks!"
    Maureen: "Well, that isn't good enough for me, wise guy! You're always late, but you never even bother calling to tell me you'll be late! I've had it with you, so you can just take off, and I'll see you around sometime!"
    Dale: "That's fine with me! You're not the only fish in the ocean, you know!"
    Maureen: "At least you know where I think you should go— go take a flying leap into the ocean!"

1.5 WHEN IS IT STUPID TO ARGUE?

In general, there's no good reason to argue if we know the thing we're arguing about is in the public records. For example, what's the point of an argument like the following one?

Patty: "Hank Aaron's 1974 batting average was really great, wasn't it?"
Carl: "Whaddaya talking about? That's the year he retired."
Patty: "No, he didn't retire then. That's the year he beat Babe Ruth's record."
Carl: "No, he retired in 1974. I remember, because he retired just after he beat Ruth's record."
Patty: "No, you're wrong."

This argument is senseless. Whether or not Aaron retired as an active baseball player in 1974 is a matter of public record. No matter how many reasons Patty and Carl give each other for their beliefs, their arguing will not change the facts. Even though Patty may convince Carl that he's wrong (or vice versa), the facts do not change. To argue about recorded facts is stupid.

On the other hand, suppose we read something and think it's <u>false</u>. Then we can argue about whether or not the record is right. Here's an example:

Sharon: "Look, it says here that Columbus discovered America in 1942."

7

Laura: "1492, not 1942."

Sharon: "No, look here. One nine four two. 1942."

Laura: "That's a misprint. It should be 1492."

Sharon: "You can't tell me that a book like this is going to get past proofreaders and everybody if it has a 450-year mistake in a date as important as this one."

In this case, Sharon has found a public record which Laura says is wrong. We notice that Sharon has given a pretty good reason for believing the book is right, but Laura hasn't given any reason for believing the book is wrong.

You may be confused by the above two paragraphs. After all, the first one says it's senseless to argue about recorded facts, and the second one says it's OK to question the record. They may appear at first to say almost opposite things. But in the first paragraph we're assuming that the record is correct (so we're assuming that the facts are recorded); and in the second paragraph we're saying that the record may be faulty (and so we're saying that the statement recorded may not be a fact).

In other words, if we agree that the answer is recorded somewhere and that the record is correct, then it's stupid to argue about the answer. But if we think the record may be wrong, then we can argue about whether or not the record really is wrong.

We can use the flow chart on the next page to help us decide whether or not it's OK to argue about something. (To read a flow chart, just follow the arrows.) Notice that the first question asks, "Is the answer recorded as fact somewhere?" In other words, if the answer is recorded somewhere simply as someone's opinion, then that record doesn't count for now. We want to know if the answer is recorded as a fact somewhere.

CLASS DISCUSSION PROBLEMS

Problems 1-3: Tell what else is needed to make the statement true. (Hint: Use the flow chart.)

1. If an answer is recorded as fact somewhere, then it's senseless to argue about the answer.
2. If you don't know whether or not an answer is recorded as fact somewhere, then it's OK to argue about the answer.
3. If an answer is on record but you think the record is wrong, then it's OK to argue about the answer.

Problems 4-9: If a question is asked, then answer it. If a statement is made, then tell whether it is true (T) or false (F).

4. Suppose you and Luke disagree about something which is a matter of record. Suppose you think the record is wrong, and Luke thinks it's right. What should you do?
5. Suppose you and Luke disagree about something which is a matter of record, and you both agree the record is faulty. What should you do?
6. You should believe everything you read.
7. Suppose you and Luke disagree about something which is a matter of record, and you both agree the record is accurate. What should you do?

8

WHEN WE DISAGREE, IS IT STUPID TO ARGUE, OR NOT?

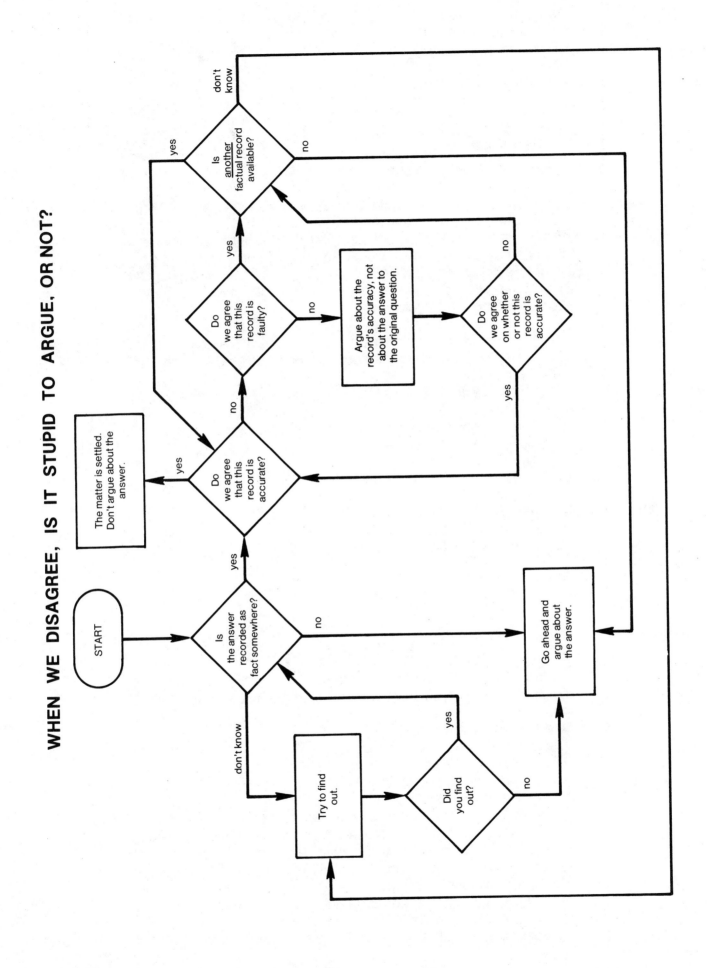

8. Suppose you and Luke disagree about something, and you can't find out whether or not the answer is recorded somewhere. What should you do?

9. Suppose you and Luke disagree about something which is a matter of opinion and so is not recorded as a fact anywhere. What should you do?

10. In the second paragraph of this section, Sharon and Laura are talking about a date printed in a book. Suppose Laura shows Sharon other records which say 1492, not 1942, and Sharon thinks the other records are all wrong. What logical arguments could Laura use to convince Sharon that the date was definitely a long time before 1942?

Problems 11-19: Tell whether or not it would be senseless to argue about the statement made. (If the answer is on record and you believe the record is right, then say "yes." If the answer is not on record, or if you believe the record is wrong, then say "no." If you don't know whether or not the answer is on record, then say "?.")

11. Suits of armor found in old ruins indicate that the average man's height then was about 5' 3", or about 160 cm.

12. A spider is an insect.

13. The President of the United States must be at least 35 years old.

14. The Constitution of the United States says that only a man can be the President of the U.S.

15. The Constitution of the United States makes it clear that only a man can be the President of the U.S.

16. Grandma Moses was a famous American architect.

17. A civilization exists under the surface of Mars.

18. Flying saucers exist.

19. Schools should be operated on a 12-month basis.

1.6 GENERAL STATEMENTS

We will say that a **general statement** is a statement about all things of a certain kind. For example, all of these are general statements:

1. All dogs have four legs.
2. No human being has six arms.
3. If a girl is 17 years old, then she's a teen-ager.
4. All birds except ostriches can fly.
5. People are illogical.

You may wonder whether or not statements 2-5 are about all things of a certain kind. The answer is yes. Another way of making statement 2 is, "If anything is a human being, then it doesn't have six arms." (That is, if we could put all human beings in one big group, we wouldn't find anything there which had six arms.) Although statement 3 is not about all girls, it is about all 17-year-old girls, so it is still a statement about all things of a certain kind— 17-year-old girls, in this case. Similarly, statement 4 is not about all birds, but it is about all <u>birds which aren't ostriches</u>. Statement 5 does not mention any exceptions, so we must assume that it applies to <u>all</u> people. (If it said, "Some people are illogical," then it would not apply to all people and so we would not call it a general statement.)

Following are some examples of statements which we will <u>not</u> call general statements. In each case, notice that the statement is <u>not</u> meant to apply to <u>all</u> cases of a certain kind.

6. Some salespeople lie about how good their products are.
7. Most novels are based on real-life situations.
8. Only a few dogs in our neighborhood are allowed to run loose.
9. Nearly everyone believes in God.
10. Many people are careless about driving habits.

Notice that we are not trying to decide whether or not statements 1-10 are true. These statements are listed simply as examples of certain kinds of statements.

CLASS DISCUSSION PROBLEMS

Answer "yes" or "no" to tell whether or not each statement is a general statement. Do <u>not</u> try to decide whether or not you agree with the statement.

1. All animals have four legs.
2. Everyone likes some things and dislikes other things.
3. Most people are honest.
4. Almost every teacher enjoys teaching.
5. No one likes a smart aleck.
6. If someone is kind to animals, then he must be a nice person.
7. Everyone knows that people watch too much television.
8. Everyone knows that most people watch too much television.
9. Anyone who doesn't know who Plato was isn't very smart.
10. Some horses are thoroughbreds.
11. Some horses are not thoroughbreds.
12. Very few roosters lay eggs.
13. No rooster lays eggs.
14. Many people would steal a million dollars if they knew they'd never be caught.
15. Almost everyone likes candy.

1.7 COUNTEREXAMPLES

A **counterexample** is a specific example which disagrees with a general statement. Several examples are given below. Each example follows the same pattern:

GS: a general statement.

C: a counterexample to the general statement.

Not C: a statement which is not a counterexample to the general statement.

In each case, the "Not C" statement will have at least one of these two properties:

1. It will not give a specific example.
2. It will not disagree with the general statement.

Example 1:

GS: All dogs have four legs.

C: John's dog was in a car accident, and it has only three legs now.

Not C: Maybe some dog was in an accident and so has only three legs left.

Example 2:

GS: All birds can fly.

C: The penguin in the zoo can't fly.

Not C: You can't fly.

Example 3:

GS: People are illogical.

C: My mother is logical.

Not C: Most mathematicians are logical.

Example 4:

GS: Anyone who doesn't know who Plato was isn't very smart.

C: My little brother doesn't know who Plato was, and he's a genius.

Not C: That isn't true, because someone could be real smart but never go to school, and so he wouldn't know about Plato.

Example 5:

GS: All people with green skin are lazy.

C: My neighbor has green skin, and she isn't lazy.

Not C: I have purple skin, and I'm not lazy.

CLASS DISCUSSION PROBLEMS

Problems 1-5: A general statement is given and is followed by lettered statements. Tell whether or not each lettered statement is a counterexample to the general statement.

1. GS: All children should be vaccinated against measles.
   a. My little sister is allergic to a lot of things, and the doctor said she shouldn't get that vaccination.
   b. That's right, because measles can be a very harmful disease.
   c. Some adults should be vaccinated against measles, too.

12

    d. The doctor said my mother shouldn't be vaccinated against measles.

2. GS: All lawyers are dishonest.
    a. My aunt is an honest lawyer.
    b. You don't even know every lawyer in the world, so you can't say that.
    c. My cousin is a policeman, and he's honest.
    d. Four of my neighbors are lawyers, and all of them are honest.

3. GS: All advertisements are exaggerated.
    a. TV ads are, but magazine ads aren't.
    b. I agree, especially about ads for children's toys.
    c. I bought a WONDER brush, and it does everything the ad said it would do.
    d. Some ads are completely truthful.

4. GS: My mother is always nagging at me about something.
    a. Yeah, mine's the same way.
    b. Your mother never nags at me.
    c. Yesterday your mother told you she liked your good report card.
    d. It's nothing personal—your mother nags at everyone.

5. GS: Everybody watches too much television these days.
    a. Some people don't have TV sets and don't watch any TV.
    b. My little brother was tired all the time, and the doctor said it was from watching too much TV.
    c. My grandfather watches soap operas on TV all morning and afternoon.
    d. My mother works, so she doesn't watch TV at all during the day.
    e. My dad never watches TV.

Problems 6-12: Each statement given is a counterexample to some general statement. Figure out what the general statement might have been and state it.

Example:
  Problem: I have brown eyes and I don't have two heads.
  Answer: All brown-eyed people have two heads.

6. I have red hair and I don't have a terrible temper.
7. The dog next door is a German Shepherd and it isn't vicious at all.
8. I keep my old car in good shape, so it isn't true that all old cars are rattletraps.
9. Mike was nice to Mr. Jeffers, but Mr. Jeffers flunked him anyhow.
10. My car gets 40 kilometers per liter of gasoline.
11. My baby sister doesn't know what a counterexample is.
12. My cousin didn't have blue eyes when he was born.

1.8 "PROOF" BY FAILURE TO FIND A COUNTEREXAMPLE

In the title above, you will notice that the first word has quotation marks around it. The quotation marks are there to show that the word is not being used correctly. They show that someone calls something a proof which isn't a proof at all. (This is like seeing a dog and calling it a cat. Just because you <u>call</u> it a cat doesn't mean that it <u>is</u> a cat.)

"Proof" by failure to find a counterexample is one kind of faulty reasoning. It happens when someone supposes that a general statement is true just because he can't find a counterexample to it.

Example 1:

Alice: "All birds can fly."

Lyle: "I've never seen a bird that couldn't fly, so you must be right."

We see that Alice has made a general statement and Lyle has agreed with her. But the <u>reason</u> Lyle has agreed seems to be just because he's never found a counterexample to Alice's statement. Lyle is using "proof" by failure to find a counterexample.

Now suppose that Lyle has never seen any kind of bird in his whole life. Then it would still be all right for him to say, "I've never seen a bird that couldn't fly." It's the truth if he says, "I've never seen a bird," so it's also the truth if he says, "I've never seen a bird that couldn't fly."

Example 2:

Helen: "All flanners have stripes."

Lyle: "I've never seen a flanner without stripes, so I guess you must be right."

("Flanner" is a word I made up.) Again Lyle is using "proof" by failure to find a counterexample. He is assuming that Helen's general statement is true because he has never found a counterexample to it.

Example 3:

Wun-Shio: "The story says that Little Red Riding Hood went to her grandmother's house."

Lyle: "Then she must not have gone to her uncle's house, because the story didn't say that she went there, too."

Here, too, Lyle is using "proof" by failure to find a counterexample. (Do you see why Lyle's statement shows this?)

CLASS DISCUSSION PROBLEMS

Problems 1-5: In each case, tell whether or not Lyle is using "proof" by failure to find a counterexample.

1. Debbie: "All handsome men are conceited."
   Lyle: "I've never seen a handsome man who wasn't conceited, so you must be right."
2. Sally: "All handsome men are conceited."
   Lyle: "That isn't true. I'm handsome, but I'm not conceited."

3. Nancy: "All invisible horses have polka dots."
   Lyle: "You must be right, because I've never seen one that didn't."
4. Juan: "No fairy tale is based on real-life characters."
   Lyle: "I've never heard of one that was, so I agree with you."
5. Rick: "This is a rotten school. No one can learn anything here."
   Lyle: "You're right. They should get some good teachers here for a change."

Problems 6-9: A general statement (GS) is given and is followed by lettered statements. For each lettered statement, tell whether it is a counterexample (C), a "proof" by failure to find a counterexample (PFFC), or neither of these (N).

6. GS: All birds can fly.
   a. Yeah, I've never seen one that couldn't.
   b. Yeah, some fish can fly, too.
   c. Naw, an elephant can't fly.
   d. Naw, baby birds can't fly.
   e. Naw, we've got a canary that can't fly.
7. GS: There are no lakes of water on the moon.
   a. That's right. If there were, then we'd have found some by now.
   b. That makes sense, since there's no water at all on the moon.
   c. There aren't now, but maybe there used to be.
   d. The moon has no rivers, either.
8. GS: No one in all of history has ever been completely honest.
   a. That's because it's so easy to be dishonest.
   b. Yeah, that story about George Washington and the cherry tree was just made up by someone.
   c. That's probably why it's always been so hard to find an honest man.
   d. Jesus was completely honest.
   e. I have to agree with you. I've never yet read about a completely honest person.
9. GS: Elves are hard to find.
   a. Maybe you're not looking in the right place.
   b. I wouldn't doubt it, since they don't even exist.
   c. There's an elf named Alfie in Ireland who's always been very friendly to me. All I do is go to his home and call his name, and he comes to the door right away.
   d. Yeah. I've looked but never found one yet.

1.9 IS YOUR THINKING STUCK IN A RUT?

Suppose Stan grows up believing that something is true. Then suppose Jake comes along and says, "Stan, forget what you were told before. I'm going to tell you something different, and I want you to think about it." Stan may find it hard not to mix up what he's always believed with what Jake tells him.

15

One part of learning to think critically is learning to separate new information from old information. We cannot begin to compare two stories until we get each one straight in our minds. It is only when we separate them that we can see if they agree or disagree with each other.

Also, no one can learn to think critically unless he learns to keep an open mind. We can't get into a rut and stay there. We can't say, "I <u>know</u> I'm right and you're wrong," unless we're willing to hear what the other person has to say and then think about it.

And another part of learning to think critically is learning to tell the difference between what is <u>really</u> <u>said</u> and what we <u>think</u> is <u>meant</u>.

Because most of us are lazy about thinking, problems 6-9 below may trick you into giving wrong answers unless you're very careful. Here are some hints to help you decide on the right answers.

1. Read each story very carefully.
2. Try to forget anything you ever heard before about the story.
3. Try to put yourself in the setting of the story when you're deciding on the answers.
4. If a classmate says your answer is wrong, listen to why he thinks it's wrong.
5. Don't change your answer unless you really think it's wrong, even if you're the only one in the class who has that answer. (Maybe you're right and everyone else is wrong.)
6. Use what you already know about general things such as what a "house" or an "apple" is. But if the story gives the word a different meaning, then you must use the story's meaning instead of what you know.

CLASS DISCUSSION PROBLEMS

1. This section lists three things a person must learn to do in order to be able to think critically. What are they?
2. Here's a test to see how well you can control your thoughts. For three minutes you are to think about anything at all EXCEPT A WHITE BEAR. YOU ARE NOT ALLOWED TO THINK ABOUT A WHITE BEAR at any time during the three minutes. Get someone to tell you when your three minutes are up. Ready? Go!
3. I've never been able to do problem 2 above, because while I'm thinking about other things, I have to remember what it is that I'm not allowed to think about. As soon as I remember that it's a white bear, then I've thought about what I'm not supposed to think about. Were <u>you</u> able to do problem 2? If not, why not?
4. Here's another test to see how well you can control your thinking. For one minute you may not think about anything EXCEPT a white bear. You cannot think about your friends or about birds or dogs or cats or polka-dotted zebras. You must think ONLY about a white bear. Get someone to tell you when your minute is up. Ready? Go!

5. I've never been able to do problem 4, either. Other things run through my mind, such as: "How much time is left?" "A car just drove by." "The phone rang." "A dog is barking outside." Were you able to do problem 4? If not, why not? [1,2]

Problems 6-9: A story is given and is followed by several statements. On the basis of the story, you are to decide whether each statement is true (T), false (F), or questionable (?). When making your decision, you must accept the story as true, and you must assume that the story uses good English. (Don't forget to use the hints given in this section for these exercises.)

6.[3]   **CINDERELLA**

Cinderella's stepmother and stepsisters disliked her. They bought themselves beautiful clothes and gifts and went to all of the important social events, but Cinderella wore rags and had to stay home. On the night of the Prince's Ball, the stepmother and stepsisters wore beautiful gowns and jewels and they left Cinderella home to clean the fireplace. But Cinderella's fairy godmother appeared and she turned Cinderella's rags into a beautiful gown. Then the fairy godmother, whose powers were granted to her for all eternity, found a pumpkin and turned it into a gold-plated automobile, and she turned a mouse into a chauffeur, and Cinderella rode to the Prince's Ball in grand style.

(1) Cinderella had more than one stepsister.
(2) Cinderella's natural mother was dead.
(3) The stepmother and stepsisters went to many social events.
(4) Cinderella's stepmother and stepsisters didn't buy any beautiful clothes for Cinderella.
(5) A pumpkin can't be turned into a gold-plated automobile.
(6) The stepmother and stepsisters disliked Cinderella.
(7) Cinderella's stepmother or stepsisters made Cinderella stay home when they went to the important social events.
(8) The stepmother and stepsisters offered to take Cinderella to the Prince's Ball with them.
(9) Cinderella walked to the Prince's Ball.
(10) Cinderella wanted to go to the Prince's Ball.
(11) The stepmother and stepsisters left Cinderella home on the night of the Prince's Ball.
(12) Cinderella rode to the Prince's Ball in a carriage drawn by six white horses.
(13) Although the stepmother and stepsisters had beautiful clothes, they never bought any clothes for themselves.
(14) The stepmother and stepsisters went only to social events which were important.
(15) Cinderella's fairy godmother was an evil witch in disguise.

---

[1] If you were able to do either problem 2 or 4, please write to me and tell me how you did it.

[2] The purpose of problems 2 and 4 above is to impress on you that we cannot always control what we think about. But a critical thinker knows this and so is more careful than ever about trying to think critically.

[3] There is no copyright either on problem 6 or on problem 7 in this section.

7.

BEAUTY AND THE BEAST

A rich merchant had three daughters. The two eldest daughters thought only of jewels, rich fabrics, and social events. But the youngest daughter, Beauty, was as kind as she was beautiful. Through a chain of circumstances, the merchant fell into the hands of Beast, who demanded that the merchant or one of the daughters come to Beast's home within two weeks, for, otherwise, Beast said he would kill the merchant and the merchant's family. Not wishing her father to have to go to Beast's house, Beauty went herself. Although Beauty thought that Beast was horrible to look at, his voice was kind and he was very intelligent. He talked for hours each day with Beauty, and he ended each day by asking Beauty to marry him. Beauty finally consented to marry him, whereupon he immediately turned into a handsome prince. Beauty and the prince were married and they lived happily ever after.

(1) Beauty's father was a rich merchant.
(2) The merchant wasn't really rich, but everyone thought the merchant was rich.
(3) Beauty was the younger of the two eldest daughters.
(4) Beauty was kind.
(5) Beauty was beautiful.
(6) The two eldest daughters were not beautiful.
(7) Maybe the two eldest daughters were beautiful.
(8) The merchant had no sons.
(9) The two eldest daughters never thought of spending a quiet evening at home.
(10) The two eldest daughters never spent a quiet evening at home.
(11) Maybe Beauty liked jewels, rich fabrics, and social events.
(12) Beauty was older than the merchant.
(13) Maybe Beauty was 70 years old.
(14) Beast had hands.
(15) Beast would have killed the whole family if the merchant or one of the daughters hadn't come to Beast's house.
(16) Beauty went to Beast's house alone.
(17) Beauty's father was already at Beast's house when Beauty arrived there.
(18) Beast was horrible to look at.
(19) Beast was ugly.
(20) Beast wanted Beauty to marry him.
(21) If Beauty hadn't agreed to marry Beast, then Beast would have killed her.
(22) Maybe Beast's voice wasn't kind.
(23) Maybe Beast wasn't very intelligent.
(24) Beast changed into a handsome prince after Beauty consented to marry Beast.
(25) Beauty didn't marry Beast.
(26) If Beauty hadn't married the prince, then she would have been an old maid.
(27) The handsome prince had been changed into Beast by sorcery.

(28) Beast was glad he had turned into a handsome prince.
(29) All girls who are kind are beautiful.
(30) All girls who are beautiful are kind.

8. ## THE EMPEROR'S NEW GARMENT

Once there was a powerful emperor who thought he was the smartest, wisest, handsomest, strongest man in the realm. He thought that anyone who disagreed with him was an inferior person, and he had such people beheaded.

One day he told his tailors, "I want something so beautiful that everyone who sees it will be stunned. If you do not make me such a garment, I will behead all of you!" The tailors hurried away and cried among themselves, "What will we do? What will we do?" Finally, one of the tailors said, "I know what to do! It is our only chance! We will tell the emperor that we are weaving for his new garment a fabric so special that only a man having the most perfect taste in clothing can appreciate its beauty. Actually, we will weave nothing at all. But the emperor will not admit that he cannot see it, so he will say he likes it." "We will do it," the tailors all cried at once, "for it is our only chance!"

The tailors did as they had agreed. At the end of six months, they sent word to the emperor that the weaving was completed and that the fabric was even more beautiful than they had dared hope. They went to the emperor and acted as though they were showing him a marvelous fabric. "Yes, yes, it is truly of stunning beauty!" cried the emperor, who, of course, saw no new fabric at all since there was no new fabric there.

So the tailors pretended to make a garment from the nonexistent fabric, and they took the nonexistent garment to the emperor. Of course, nobody ever dared to tell the emperor that he was wearing only his underwear whenever he "wore his new garment," for to say such a thing would mean instant death. But when the emperor wasn't around, almost everyone was laughing at him for being such a fool.

(1) The emperor was smart.
(2) The emperor was wise.
(3) The emperor was handsome.
(4) The emperor was strong.
(5) The emperor was powerful.
(6) The emperor thought that he was superior to some people.
(7) The emperor believed that all people are equal.
(8) The emperor beheaded people who disagreed with him.
(9) The emperor had only one tailor.
(10) The emperor would have beheaded the tailors if they had not made him the special garment he demanded.
(11) The tailors had no reasonable course of action other than the one they took.
(12) The tailors could have made a fabric which would have satisfied the emperor's demand.
(13) The tailors were afraid to tell the emperor that he had made an impossible demand.
(14) The tailors lied to the emperor.
(15) The tailors didn't really lie to the emperor. He just misinterpreted what they told him.

(16) In the story, the emperor's tailors did not make a garment for him.

(17) Maybe the special fabric in the story really was so beautiful that only the emperor could see it.

(18) Maybe the tailors really did make a fabric so beautiful that only the emperor could see it.

(19) At the end of the story, most people thought the emperor was a fool.

(20) When the emperor thought he was wearing his new garment, everyone was afraid to tell him that he was wearing only his underwear.

(21) If anyone had told the emperor he was wearing only his underwear when he (the emperor) thought he was wearing his new garment, the emperor would have had that person beheaded.

(22) The emperor was blind.

9. ## THE UGLY DUCKLING

A duck laid some eggs and then sat on them to keep them warm so they would hatch. One day she left them to look for food. When she returned, she thought one of the eggs looked strange. (There was one more egg there now, but she was unable to count.) She sat on the eggs again, and finally the eggs hatched. The original eggs hatched first. The mother duck always told the truth, and she told each duckling how lovely it was. When the extra egg hatched, the mother duck was aghast at the thing which emerged. She shouted at it, "How could I have hatched something as horrible as you?! I am going to name you Ugly!"

The mother duck always fed the ducklings first, and Ugly got only the leftovers. When her neighbors came calling, she made Ugly hide so that her neighbors would not know about him. She taught her ducklings how to swim, and she took them swimming in the lake, leaving Ugly home by himself. He cried because he was so lonely. His mother never talked to him except to tell him that he was ugly and that she was ashamed of him and that if anyone found out about him it would disgrace her.

Eventually Ugly taught himself how to swim. He was swimming alone one day when some men came along. "Look at that beautiful young swan!" exclaimed one man. "Yes! Isn't it marvelous?" cried another. Ugly looked around to see who they were talking about, but only he and the men were there. "Come with us," one of the men said to Ugly, "to a place where there are other lovely creatures like yourself." Ugly went with the men to a place where other swans lived. Every day people came by and told Ugly that he and the other swans were gorgeous.

Ugly was much happier in his new home, but it was a long, long time before he believed that he really _was_ beautiful and not ugly.

(1) When the new egg was added to the mother duck's nest, one of the original eggs was replaced by another duck egg.

20

(2) The mother duck did not know how to count.

(3) The mother duck must not have gone to school very long, for otherwise she would have learned how to count.

(4) When the mother duck was hatching the eggs, someone usually brought food to her.

(5) The mother duck thought that Ugly was a duck.

(6) Ugly was a duck.

(7) The mother duck thought Ugly ugly.

(8) The mother duck was ashamed of Ugly.

(9) The mother duck told Ugly she was ashamed of him, but maybe she wasn't really ashamed of him.

(10) The mother duck did not want her neighbors to find out about Ugly.

(11) The mother duck didn't care whether or not outsiders (non-neighbors) found out about Ugly.

(12) If anyone had found out about Ugly, the mother duck would have been disgraced.

(13) The mother duck hated Ugly.

(14) The mother duck taught Ugly how to swim.

(15) Sometimes the mother duck let Ugly go swimming with her and the ducklings.

(16) When Ugly learned how to swim, the mother duck hoped he would swim away.

(17) The mother duck was glad that Ugly learned how to swim.

(18) Ugly was lonely before the men found him.

(19) There were at least two men who came along and saw Ugly swimming alone.

(20) There were more than two men who came along and saw Ugly swimming alone.

(21) Ugly went willingly with the men who found him swimming alone.

(22) The men who found Ugly swimming alone thought that Ugly was a swan.

(23) Ugly was a swan.

(24) Maybe Ugly wasn't either a swan or a duck.

(25) All the people who saw Ugly and the other swans thought them beautiful.

(26) Some of the people who saw Ugly and the other swans thought them beautiful.

(27) Ugly was not lonely when he lived with the swans.

(28) Ugly was a male.

(29) Ugly never did really believe that he wasn't ugly.

(30) Beauty lies in the eye of the beholder.

10. For this problem, a story is given but is not followed by any statements. You are to make up at least five statements to be judged "T," "F," or "?" by your classmates. Try to make up at least one statement which you think many of your classmates will get wrong.

THE PRINCESS AND THE FROG

While running one day, a beautiful princess fell into a well. She cried because she was unable to get out alone. A frog came along and said he could get her out if she would do him a favor in return. The frog said that he was really a handsome prince who had been cast under a spell by a witch. He said that if the princess would agree to kiss him, then he would get her out of the well. He said the spell would be broken if she would kiss him. The princess agreed to kiss the frog if he got her out of the well. The frog got the princess out of the well and then said, "Now you must kiss me." The princess turned up her nose and said, "You've got to be kidding! You are too ugly to be kissed by a beautiful princess like me!" The frog said, "I kid you not. A princess always keeps her word, and you gave me your word." So the princess kissed the frog, and he turned into a handsome prince.

1.10 CLASS DISCUSSION PROBLEMS AND QUESTIONS FOR CHAPTER REVIEW

1. Following are some paragraphs about the way someone thought. For each paragraph, tell whether or not the person was thinking critically.
   a. A famous biology professor told Pam that in some cases the male animal of the species is the one who lays the eggs. Pam had always thought the female of any species was the one who laid the eggs, but she figured that the professor was famous and so should know what he was talking about, and so she believed him.
   b. George was doing a reading assignment when he found a word he didn't know. He looked up the word in the dictionary.
   c. Some people were talking about whose pictures are on paper money, and the question came up of whose picture is on a $1000 bill. Valerie said one thing and Rita said another, and each tried to convince the other that she was wrong.
   d. Eileen told Kay that a blue-eyed mother and a brown-eyed father would have three blue-eyed children for every brown-eyed child. Kay didn't know what determines the color of a person's eyes, but she said that Eileen had to be wrong, since the mother and father must have an equal share in this.
2. What's the difference between a disagreement and an argument? between an argument and a fight?
3. What should you do if a question comes up and you don't know whether or not the answer is recorded as a fact somewhere?
4. Which of the following are general statements?
   a. Birch trees have white bark.
   b. You're always saying things like that.
   c. All of my teachers pick on me.
   d. Most of the new cars are lemons.
   e. Chocolate makes my face break out.
   f. She never wants to let anyone else do any talking.
   g. Almost every kid on my block is selfish.

    h.   I never know whether or not I'm doing the right thing.
    i.   He's always trying to impress people.
    j.   No one knows the answer to that question.
    k.   Someone usually manages to mess things up.

5. Decide whether or not each statement is a counterexample to the statement, "These scissors don't cut anything right."
   a. I just now cut a piece of paper with them, and they worked fine.
   b. They should be sharpened, and then they'd work OK.
   c. That's the way cheap scissors are.
   d. That's because they're right-handed scissors, and you're left-handed.
   e. You shouldn't say that. You'll hurt their feelings, and then they won't cut at all.
   f. They worked OK an hour ago when I used them to cut some shingles.

6. You are given the sentence, "All dogs can be trained." Which of the following statements use "proof" by failure to find a counterexample?
   a. Yes, dogs are easily tamed, so they can be trained, too.
   b. No, my dog is too vicious to be trained.
   c. Yes, given the right trainer, any dog can be trained.
   d. Yes, I've never yet heard of a dog which couldn't be trained.
   e. I can't think of a counterexample, so you must be right.
   f. I can't think of a counterexample, but I'll bet there's a dog somewhere in the world which can't be trained.

7. Accept the story as true, and tell whether each statement following the story is "T," "F," or "?."

   The sky was blue and contained great white fluffy clouds. A bird soared gracefully above Ramon as he lay on the short, thick, soft grass. Watching the bird, Ramon thought, "How wonderful it would be to fly like that!"
   (1) The sky contained at least two clouds.
   (2) The sky did not contain any small clouds.
   (3) Ramon saw at least two birds as he lay on the grass thinking.
   (4) Ramon did not think there was anything special about being able to fly as the bird was flying.
   (5) Ramon liked to watch the bird soar.
   (6) In the story, Ramon was lying at least 50 feet above the ground.
   (7) Ramon was blind.
   (8) Maybe Ramon was a cat.
   (9) Maybe Ramon wasn't a cat.
   (10) Maybe the sky wasn't blue.

CHAPTER 2

INTRODUCTION TO LOGIC

2.1   SYMBOLS USED IN THIS CHAPTER

2.2   ''OR'' SENTENCES AND THEIR TRUTH VALUES

2.3   ''AND'' SENTENCES AND THEIR TRUTH VALUES

2.4   DOUBLE NEGATIVES AND MULTIPLE ''∼'' SIGNS

2.5   NECESSARY AND SUFFICIENT CONDITIONS

2.6   ''IF-THEN'' SENTENCES

2.7   TRUTH VALUES OF ''IF-THEN'' SENTENCES

2.8   PROPOSITION, CONVERSE, INVERSE, CONTRAPOSITIVE

2.9   SUBSTITUTION OF CONVERSE OR INVERSE FOR ITS PROPOSITION

2.10   ''ONLY IF'' SENTENCES AND THEIR TRUTH VALUES

2.11   ARGUMENTS, PREMISES, AND CONCLUSIONS

2.12   CLASS DISCUSSION PROBLEMS AND QUESTIONS FOR CHAPTER REVIEW

2.1 SYMBOLS USED IN THIS CHAPTER

Among other things, the study of logic will teach you rules to use for certain kinds of sentences. A rule changes when the kind of sentence changes, so you should learn to identify the kind of sentence you're using. It will turn out that the rule for a sentence will apply regardless of the words in the sentence, and it will be easier to talk about the sentence if we use symbols instead of words.

First, we will agree to use a capital block letter in place of all the words needed for a <u>simple complete thought.</u>

Example 1:
Suppose we want to write, "If Aaron leaves right now, then Bert will give him a ride home."
Put A = Aaron leaves right now.
Put B = Bert will give Aaron a ride home.
Then write, "If A, then B."

We see that "If A, then B" is easier to identify as being an "if-then" sentence than the sentence with all the words left in.

Some people might prefer to use more than one capital block letter to express a thought.

Example 2:
Suppose we want to write, "If the animal is a tiger, then it has big claws."
Put AT = the animal is a tiger.
Put ABC = the animal has big claws.
Then write, "If AT, then ABC."

> **Symbol:**
> A capital block letter (A, B, C, and so on) is used in place of a complete thought.

We will use "~" to mean "not" or "it is false that" or "it is not the case that."

Example 3:
Suppose we want to write, "If Dal-Chin doesn't leave right now, then Pedro will give her a ride home."
Put D = Dal-Chin leaves right now.
Put P = Pedro will give Dal-Chin a ride home.
Then write, "If ~ D, then P."

If we didn't know what the words were for that last sentence, we'd read it as, "If not D, then P." We could also read it as, "If D is false, then P."

Example 4:
Suppose we want to write, "Either that animal has big claws, or it's not a tiger."
Put ABC = that animal has big claws.
Put AT = that animal is a tiger.
Then write, "ABC or ~ AT."

Notice that we left out the word "either" in the last sentence. That's because it isn't really needed—the sentence means exactly the same thing whether or not we include the word "either" in it. We can read that last sentence as, "ABC or not AT."

Symbol:

$\sim$ = "not" or "it is false that" or "it is not the case that."

"If-then" sentences are used so often in logic that we use the symbol "→" in place of the words "if" and "then."

Example 5:

The result of Example 1 can be written as "A→B."

The result of Example 2 can be written as "AT→ABC."

The result of Example 3 can be written as "$\sim$ D→P."

"A→B" is read, "A implies B," or, "If A, then B."

Symbol:

→ = implies

P→Q = P implies Q.

P→Q = If P, then Q.

CLASS DISCUSSION PROBLEMS

Problems 1-7: Tell whether or not the symbol is being used correctly.

1. Put EW = an elephant has wings.
2. Put E = elephant.
3. If P→Q.
4. If R,→S.
5. $\sim$ S if R.
6. $\sim$ C→D.
7. $\sim$ (C→D).

Problems 8-17: Decide whether each sentence is true (T) or false (F).

8. "If F→G" is an incomplete sentence.
9. "$\sim$ F→$\sim$ G" can be read, "Not F implies not G."
10. "$\sim$ F→$\sim$ G" can be read, "If not F, then not G."
11. "$\sim$ F→ $\sim$ G" can be read, "If F is false, then G is false."
12. "If P, then Q" has the same meaning as "If Q, then P."
13. "If P, then Q" has the same meaning as "Q if P."
14. "If P, then Q" has the same meaning as "Q implies P."
15. "$\sim$ (R→S)" can be read as "It is false that R implies S."
16. "$\sim$ (R→S)" can be read as "Not R implies S."
17. In the sentence, "U X," the "U"may stand for an incomplete thought.

Problems 18-24: Tell what, if anything, is wrong with what the student did.

18. Rose wanted to write, "If Ernie goes, then Eva will go," so she put E = "Ernie goes," and she put E = "Eva will go," and she wrote, "E→E."
19. Mona wanted to write, "If Ernie goes, then Eva will go," so she put ER = "Ernie goes," and she put EV = "Eva will go," and she wrote "ER EV."
20. Ruby wanted to write, "If Ernie goes, then Eva will go," so she put ER = "Ernie," and she put EV = "Eva," and she wrote, "ER→EV."
21. Amos wanted to write, "If I go, then you won't go, and if I don't go, then you'll go." He put I = "I go," and he put Y = "you'll go." He wrote, "I→$\sim$ Y, and $\sim$ I→Y."

27

22. Hshan-Wun wanted to write the same sentence Amos wrote. Hshan-Wun put A = "if I go, then you won't go," and he put B = "if I don't go, then you'll go." He wrote, "A and B."
23. Bernice wanted to write, "A does not imply B," so she wrote, "A → ~ B."
24. Elaine saw the sentence, "P if Q." She decided that it could written, "P ← Q." She didn't like to have the arrow pointing the opposite way like that, so she rewrote the sentence as, "Q → P."

Problems 25-33: Choosing from the following list of substitutions, restate each problem in symbolized form. Don't worry about whether or not the words of the problem make sense to you.

  D = dinosaurs exist
  I = invisible horses are polka-dotted
  E = elephants have wings

25. If dinosaurs exist, then invisible horses are polka-dotted.
26. If dinosaurs exist, then dinosaurs do not exist. So dinosaurs do not exist.
27. If it is false that invisible horses are polka-dotted, then dinosaurs don't exist.
28. It is false that if invisible horses are polka-dotted, then dinosaurs don't exist.
29. If invisible horses aren't polka-dotted, then it's false that dinosaurs exist.
30. If elephants have wings or dinosaurs exist, then invisible horses are polka-dotted.
31. Either elephants have wings, or if dinosaurs exist then invisible horses are polka-dotted.
32. If it is false that elephants don't have wings, then dinosaurs exist.
33. Either dinosaurs don't exist, or elephants don't have wings. But if elephants don't have wings, then invisible horses are not polka-dotted. However, invisible horses are polka-dotted. So dinosaurs don't exist.

2.2 "OR" SENTENCES AND THEIR TRUTH VALUES

You've already seen "or" sentences in section 2.1. An "or" sentence is a sentence which gives us a choice of two thoughts. Following are some "or" sentences:

1. Either today is the 4th of July or today is Christmas Day.
2. The word "respect" means "hold in high regard" or "think highly of."[1]
3. Either you have three arms or you don't have three arms.
4. Either you don't have five legs or you have five legs.
5. Either you are a human being or you are a machine made of plastic.

---

[1] Sentence 2 is written as we would usually say it. In logic, it would be written, "The word 'respect' means 'hold in high regard,' or the word 'respect' means 'think highly of.'" In order to have a choice of two thoughts, each thought must, of course, be a complete thought.

6. Most teenagers like hamburger or pizza.[1]
7. You weigh 900 kilograms or you are 287 years old.
8. Either George Washington was born before Columbus, or Marco Polo was an explorer.

CLASS DISCUSSION PROBLEMS

Problems 1-5: Choosing from the following list of substitutions, restate each sentence in symbolized form.

T = you had your forehead tattooed
Y = you wanted to have your forehead tattooed
P = your parents let you have your forehead tattooed

1. Either you had your forehead tattooed or your parents didn't let you do it.
2. Either you had your forehead tattooed or you didn't want to do it.
3. Either your parents let you have your forehead tattooed or you didn't have it done.

---

[1]Sentence 6, too, is written as we would usually say it. In logic, it would be written, "Most teenagers like hamburger, or most teenagers like pizza."

[2]When we say that a sentence is of a certain form, we mean that substitutions can be made in it so that it ends up looking like the sentence in the form we specify. For example, ~R or S is of the form P or Q, for we can put P = ~R, Q = S. As another example, ~(A and B) or ~(~C or ~D) is of the form P or Q, for we can put P = ~(A and B), Q = ~(~C or ~D). You will notice that P and Q do not necessarily stand for simple thoughts in this case. In practice, we still write that last sentence as, "~(A and B) or ~(~C or ~D)," but we think of it as, "P or Q," so that we recognize that the rules for "or" sentences apply to it.

[3]Parents have been known to object to this. If, after your usual temper tantrum over not getting your own way, your parents still don't like the idea, explain this to your teacher and ask to be excused from having your forehead tattooed. Have your paper from Class Exercise 3(b) above with you at all times, however.

4. Either your parents let you have your forehead tattooed or you didn't want it done.
5. If you didn't want to have your forehead tattooed, then you didn't have it done.

Problems 6-10: Choosing your own substitution symbols, do two things for each problem:
   a. Tell exactly what your substitutions are.
   b. Restate the problem in symbolized form.
6. You read the comics or the front page of the newspaper.
7. Either you're not serious or you're awfully dense today.
8. Either the SUPER-8 is a good car or I'll eat my hat.
9. Either you're good at team sports or you don't like them at all.
10. If you can't make up your mind, then you're indecisive.

Problems 11-20: Using the tattoo on your forehead [1] or the paper you saved from the Class Exercises in this section, tell the truth value of each statement.
11. Either invisible horses have polka dots, or you're a human being.
12. Either you understand this material or you need more time to think about it.
13. You're either a girl or a boy.
14. You went swimming yesterday or you stayed home.
15. You went to school today, or you stayed home.
16. Either you brushed your teeth this morning or you have bad breath.
17. You took a shower or a bath this morning.
18. You find these problems easy to do or you don't understand them completely.
19. Either you're wearing socks now or your feet are dirty.
20. Either you like police officers or you think you have a good reason for not liking them.

2.3 "AND" SENTENCES AND THEIR TRUTH VALUES

An "and" sentence is a sentence which has two thoughts connected by the word "and." We can use the same examples as in section 2.2, changing each "or" to "and" and leaving out the word "either" where it appears.

1. Today is the 4th of July and today is Christmas Day.
2. The word "respect" means "hold in high regard" and "think highly of."
3. You have three arms and you don't have three arms.
4. You don't have five legs and you have five legs.
5. You are a human being and you are a machine made of plastic.
6. Most teenagers like hamburger and pizza.
7. You weigh 900 kilograms and you are 287 years old.
8. George Washington was born before Columbus, and Marco Polo was an explorer.

[1] I forgot to tell you to have it tattooed on backwards so that when you hold up a mirror to read it, it reads the right way. Sorry about that!

We see that some of the sentences which were true when we used "or" are not true when we use "and." To find out about the truth value of an "and" sentence, we'll go through the same procedure we used for an "or" sentence.

CLASS EXERCISES

1. Write the numerals 1-8 in a column. Draw lines to make three more columns. Head the first column "TV," the second column "P," and the third column "Q."
   a. In the "TV" column, write the truth value of each of the eight "and" sentences above.
   b. Each of the "and" sentences is of the form "P and Q." For each sentence, write the truth value of P in the "P" column, and write the truth value of Q in the "Q" column. (Your "P" and "Q" columns here should have exactly the same entries as your "P" and "Q" columns for the section 2.2 Class Exercises.)
2. Look for a <u>pattern</u> in your three columns to tell you when an "and" sentence is true and when an "and" sentence is false.
3. a. How many ways are there for an "and" sentence to be true? How many ways are there for an "and" sentence to be false?
   b. On a separate sheet of paper, write and complete this sentence: "The sentence 'P and Q' is true if and only if _____." Take the paper home with you tonight and have the sentence tattooed on your forehead just underneath the "or" sentence tattoo. Remember to have it tattooed backwards this time so that you can read it easily when you look in a mirror. Leave room for another tattoo later.

CLASS DISCUSSION PROBLEMS

Problems 1-5: Using the substitutions shown below, restate each sentence in symbolized form.

A = all ads are exaggerated
S = some products work the way their ads say they will

1. All ads are exaggerated, and it is false that some products work the way their ads say they will.
2. It is false that all ads are exaggerated, and some products work the way their ads say they will.
3. Some ads are not exaggerated, and some products work the way their ads say they will.
4. If all ads are exaggerated, then it is false that some products work the way their ads say they will.
5. Some ads are not exaggerated, and no product works the way its ad says it will.

Problems 6-10: Choosing your own substitution symbols, do two things for each problem:
  a. Tell exactly what your substitutions are.
  b. Restate the problem in symbolized form.
  6. You're good-looking and you have a good personality.
  7. You're smart and you're witty.
  8. You like red cars and black motorcycles.
  9. The weather was rotten today, and the mail got here late.
 10. A stapler and a box of paper clips are handy things to have.

Problems 11-20: Tell the truth value of each statement.
 11. You have purple hair and green eyes.
 12. You are 3 meters tall and you weigh less than 1 kilogram.
 13. Some snowmobiles are dangerous, and so are some cars.
 14. Ice skating is fun, and so is swimming.
 15. The sky is blue and cloudless.
 16. Outer space is very cold and the sun is very hot.
 17. Some students are apple-polishers, and some teachers are easily fooled.
 18. All teachers do a good job of teaching, and some teachers think they're smart.
 19. You've never been on any of the stars in Orion, or you wouldn't be here now.
 20. You can't fly under your own power, and you're either lying to me or fooling yourself by telling me that you can.

2.4 DOUBLE NEGATIVES AND MULTIPLE "∼" SIGNS

Study the following conversation:

Leah: "It's false that I'm not going."
Gail: "You mean you're not going?"
Leah: "No, I said, 'It's <u>false</u> that I'm not going.'"
Gail: "Oh, then you're going?"
Leah: "Sure. If it's <u>false</u> that I'm <u>not</u> going, then it must be true that I'm going."
Gail: "It would've been a lot simpler if you'd just said that you were going."

We see that Leah used a double negative in her first sentence, and the double negative did not serve a useful purpose. In fact, as Gail said, the double negative just made Leah's statement harder to understand than it should have been.

If we put L = "Leah is going," then we can symbolize the conversation:

> Leah: " ~~ L."
> Gail: "You mean ~L?"
> Leah: "No, I said, ' ~~ L."
> Gail: "Oh, then L?"
> Leah: "Sure, if ~~ L, then L."
> Gail: "It would've been a lot simpler if you'd just said that L."

We see that the effect of two consecutive[1] "~" signs is to cancel each other.

Here are some other examples:

Example 1:
> Statement: It's false that the sky is not clear.
> Simplified meaning: The sky is clear.
> Symbolization: Let C = the sky is clear. Then " ~~ C" is the same as "C."

Example 2:
> Statement: It isn't true that this isn't good.
> Simplified meaning: This is good.
> Symbolization: Let S = "this is good." Then " ~~ S" is the same as "S."

In both examples and in the conversation between Leah and Gail, you will notice that all of the double negatives were of the form, "It is false that [something] is not [such-and-such]." (Of course, "it isn't true" means the same as "it is false that.") It is always safe to cancel the double negatives in this case.

However, there are some cases where it may appear that a statement is the negation of (or the "~" of) another statement and it is not at all the negation.

Example 3:
> Statement: This is good.
> Negation: This is not good.
> Not negation: This is bad.

"Bad" is not the logical negation of "good," for something may be good, bad, or indifferent. Therefore, if we say something is not good, we say that it is either bad or indifferent, not simply that it is bad. (And we do not say simply that it is indifferent.)

Example 4:
> Statement: I like him.
> Negation: I don't like him.
> Not negation: I dislike him.

We may like someone or dislike him or be indifferent about him. For example, we neither like nor dislike someone we've never heard of.

---

[1] Two things are said to be **consecutive** if one follows immediately after the other with nothing else coming between them.
Example A: The "~" signs are consecutive in the sentence, " ~~A."
Example B: The "~" signs are _not_ consecutive in the sentence," ~ (~P or Q)."
Example C: The "~" signs are _not_ consecutive in the sentence," ~ P or ~ Q."
Example D: The "~" signs are _not_ consecutive in the sentence, "~P→~Q."

CLASS DISCUSSION PROBLEMS

Problems 1-10: Each problem is a statement in symbolized form. Simply the statement if it is possible to do so; otherwise, answer "simplified" to show that the statement is already in its simplest form.

Example 1:
   Problem: $\sim\sim$ P
   Answer: P

Example 2:
   Problem: $\sim$ R
   Answer: simplified

1. $\sim\sim$ P or Q
2. $\sim(\sim$P or Q)
3. $\sim\sim$ P → Q
4. $\sim(\sim$P → Q)
5. $\sim\sim$ S or $\sim\sim$ T
6. $\sim(\sim$ S or $\sim\sim$ T)
7. $\sim$A → $\sim$B
8. $\sim\sim\sim$ R
9. $\sim\sim\sim$ R → $\sim$U
10. $\sim\sim\sim\sim$ X

Problems 11-21: Using words, simplify the statement if it is possible to do so without changing the meaning; otherwise, answer "simplified" to show that the statement cannot be simplified. (Hint: If you have trouble deciding, try symbolizing the statement.)

11. It is false that it isn't raining now.
12. It is false that I dislike him.
13. It is false that I don't like him.
14. Either it is false that I don't like red cars, or I don't like green cars.
15. It is false that either I don't like red cars or I don't like green cars.
16. If it's false that I'm not going, then I won't stay home.
17. It's false that if I'm not going then I won't stay home.
18. It isn't true that it's false that I don't like him.
19. It isn't true that it's false that it's not the case that I don't like him.
20. Phyllis didn't bring no pencil today.
21. Phyllis didn't bring any pencil today.

2.5 NECESSARY AND SUFFICIENT CONDITIONS

Two things might be related in such a way that the first thing is enough to cause the second thing, or the first thing is enough to guarantee us that the second thing is true. In this case, we say that the first thing is a **sufficient condition** for the second thing, and the second thing is a **necessary condition** for the first thing.

Example 1:

We know that we must have clouds in order to have rain. All of the following statements are equivalent:[1]

a. We must have clouds in order to have rain.
b. We have clouds whenever we have rain.
c. There are clouds if there is rain.
d. If there is rain, then there are clouds.
e. Having rain is enough to guarantee us that we have clouds.
f. Having rain is a sufficient reason for us to conclude that we have clouds.
g. Rain is a sufficient condition for clouds.
h. Having clouds is necessary in order to have rain.
i. Clouds are a necessary condition for rain.

Do not confuse a <u>sufficient condition</u> with a <u>necessary condition</u>, for the two ideas are not the same.

Example 2:

a. Rain is a sufficient condition for clouds.
b. Rain is not a necessary condition for clouds. (That is, it is not necessary to have rain in order to have clouds.)
c. Clouds are a necessary condition for rain.
d. Clouds are not a sufficient condition for rain. (That is, we can have clouds without having rain.)

Example 3:

We know that a rectangle is a four-sided figure.

a. Having a rectangle is a sufficient condition for having a four-sided figure.
b. Having a rectangle is not a necessary condition for having a four-sided figure.
c. Having a four-sided figure is a necessary condition for having a rectangle.
d. Having a four-sided figure is not a sufficient condition for having a rectangle.

To summarize, all of the following are equivalent statements:

1. If P, then Q.
2. $P \rightarrow Q$.
3. Q if P.
4. P is a <u>sufficient condition</u> for Q.
5. Q is a <u>necessary condition</u> for P.

CLASS DISCUSSION PROBLEMS

1. Explain in your own words what is meant by saying, "R is a sufficient condition for S."
2. Explain in your own words what is meant by saying, "T is a necessary condition for U."
3. Substituting words from everyday life for P, Q, R, etc., give an example of the statement,
   a. P is a sufficient condition for Q.
   b. R is not a sufficient condition for S.

---

[1]**Equivalent statements** are two (or more) statements which have the same logical meaning. They may be freely substituted for each other. In everyday writing and conversation, we choose whichever one of the two statements seems to sound better to us at the moment.

c. T is a necessary condition for U.

d. V is not a necessary condition for W.

e. X is both necessary and sufficient for Y.

f. A is neither necessary nor sufficient for B.

4. If you know that R is a sufficient condition for S, <u>must</u> it also be true that S is a necessary condition for R? Support your answer.

5. If you know that Y is a necessary condition for Z, <u>must</u> it also be true that Z is a sufficient condition for Y? Support your answer.

6. If R is a sufficient condition for S, must R also be a necessary condition for S? Support your answer.

7. If Y is a necessary condition for Z, must Y also be a sufficient condition for Z? Support your answer.

8. If P is both necessary and sufficient for Q, must Q be both necessary and sufficient for P? Support your answer.

Problems 9-15: For each problem, state as many things as you can about necessary and sufficient conditions. Use your knowledge of the world.

Example:

Problem: Every tree is a plant.

Answer: Being a tree is a sufficient condition for being a plant.
Being a tree is not a necessary condition for being a plant.
Being a plant is a necessary condition for being a tree.
Being a plant is not a sufficient condition for being a tree.

9. Every dog is an animal.

10. A pencil is a writing instrument.

11. A computer is a machine.

12. All attorneys are college graduates.

13. All fire fighters are brave.

14. If someone is a college professor, then that person is intelligent.

15. A triangle has at least three sides.

2.6 "IF-THEN" SENTENCES

An "if-then" sentence is a sentence in which two possibilities are related so that the occurrence of one promises the occurrence of the other. The word "if" must appear in the sentence.[1] The word "then" may appear in the sentence, or it may not appear and may be taken for granted from the nature of the sentence. Following are examples of "if-then" sentences:

1. If we have rain, then we have clouds.

2. If Art dissects a frog, then he is very nervous.

3. Yoshiko laughs if she hears a joke.

4. Susan shivers whenever she's cold.

---

[1] Logically, an equivalent word may be substituted for "if." Examples are "when," "whenever," and "provided that." So the sentence, "When you're ready, then I'll be ready," is considered logically to be an "if-then" sentence.

5. Whenever it's Saturday, Al is glad.
6. Mrs. Andrews always yells at her students when they don't pay attention.
7. When Peter has too much homework to do, he gets upset.
8. Nat cries when he sees a sad movie.
9. If Rosemary goes outside, she has to wear sunglasses.
10. Provided that Esther gets an A on a test, she is happy.

In logic, we like to be consistent about the way we write "if-then" sentences, so we always write such a sentence as "P → Q" —that is, "If P, then Q."

2.7 TRUTH VALUES OF "IF-THEN" SENTENCES

Suppose Hal points to a triangle and says, "If this is a triangle, then it has four sides." We all know that a triangle has exactly three sides, so we know that Hal lied to us.

Putting P = "this is a triangle" and Q = "this has four sides," Hal has made a false "P → Q" statement. We were told that he pointed to a triangle, so P was true. But we also know that a triangle doesn't have four sides, so Q was false. In this case, "P→Q" was false when P was true and Q was false.

A little thought will convince us that "P → Q" is always false when P is true and Q is false. Looking back to section 2.5, we see that saying "P→Q" is the same as saying, "P is a sufficient condition for Q," or, "Having P is enough to guarantee us that we have Q." So we can't very well say that having P is enough to guarantee us Q and then turn around and say we have P but not Q. Therefore, we can make

Statement 1: P→Q is false if P is true and Q is false.

Using a similar line of reasoning, it also follows that if P and Q are both true, then "P → Q" is true. Again, suppose Hal points to a triangle and says, "If this is a triangle, then _____."
We see that the only way Hal's sentence will be true is if he finishes it with a true "then" part. So we will make

37

Statement 2: P→Q is true if P is true and Q is true.

Both of Statements 1 and 2 above suppose that P is true. But if P is false, then what's the truth value of P→Q? Logicians disagree on this. In this case, most logicians say that P→Q is true, but some say that P→Q is neither true nor false. We will agree with the majority on this one.

To show how this decision can be justified, we reason as follows: A statement P→Q is a guarantee. Whoever makes that guarantee is either lying or he isn't. But if he isn't lying, then he must be telling the truth.[1] For example, suppose someone says, "If it rains tomorrow, then I'm not going fishing." He hasn't said anything about what he'll do or not do if it <u>doesn't</u> rain tomorrow. So suppose tomorrow comes along and it doesn't rain. Regardless of whether or not he goes fishing, we can't say he lied to us. So we will assume he told the truth.

What we now have is

Statement 3: P→Q is true if P is false.

If we combine the information in Statements 1, 2, and 3, we can make this truth table:

If P is	and if Q is	then P→Q is
T	T	T
T	F	F
F	T	T
F	F	T

This truth table makes it easier to see that the following sentence is right:

> The sentence "P→Q" is false if and only if P is true and Q is false.

If you have that one tattooed on your forehead along with the other two, you won't have to remember where it is in the book when you want to remember what it says.

CLASS DISCUSSION PROBLEMS

Problems 1-14: Using your knowledge of the world, tell the truth value of each sentence ("T," "F," or "?"). If your answer is "?" then tell what you need to know and tell how it would affect the truth value. Assume that "you" means <u>you</u>.

Example:

Problem: If flanners have stripes, then you have green hair.

Answer: ?. I need to know whether or not flanners have stripes. I don't have green hair, so if flanners have stripes, the sentence is false; and if flanners don't have stripes, then the sentence is true.

1. If today is the 4th of July, then you have green hair.
2. If today is not the 4th of July, then you have green hair.
3. If today is the 4th of July, then you don't have green hair.

[1]This is the point about which logicians disagree. It is possible to make a statement which is neither true nor false. For example, suppose someone says, "The statement I am making right now is a lie." Think about that one. That statement, however, is not an "if-then" sentence, and we are going to say that an "if-then" sentence has to be either true or false.

4. If today is not the 4th of July, then you don't have green hair.
5. If flanners have stripes, then most teenagers like pizza.
6. If you are 500 years old, then you are in the third grade.
7. If you have a mother or father, then you are not an orphan.
8. You're not very wise if you're only 5 years old.
9. All trees have brown bark if some doctors are women.
10. If your school has a swimming pool, then it has a football team.
11. Your school has a swimming pool if it has a football team.
12. The SUPER-8 is the best car on the market if there are no other cars on the market.
13. Invisible horses are polka-dotted, provided that live elephants have wings.
14. You're open-minded when you're thinking critically.

Problems 15-18: Each problem is an "if-then" statement which has either the "if" part or the "then" part missing. Make up two sets of words for each missing part—one set of words to make the sentence true, and the other set to make the sentence false. If it is not possible to do this, tell why not.

Example:
Problem: If everybody knows what a counterexample is, then _____.

Answer: Not possible. The "if" part is false, which means that the sentence is true regardless of what the "then" part is.

15. If_____, then all homes have three TV sets.
16. If_____, then Mark Spitz won seven gold medals in the Olympics.
17. If nobody likes swimming, then _____.
18. If bamboo is a plant, then_____.

Problems 19-31: Do <u>not</u> use your knowledge of the world. Accept each sentence as true, and tell the truth value ("T," "F," or "?") of the underlined part(s). Be ready to explain your answers.

Example:
Problem: If <u>teenagers are usually nice</u>, then all teachers like to teach.
It is false that all teachers like to teach.
Answer: F.
Explanation: The problem is of the form
N→T
~T
and we are told that both sentences are true. Then T must be false. But since T is false, and since N → T is true, we must have that N is false.

19. If <u>all triangles have four sides</u>, then all circles are lopsided. Not all circles are lopsided.
20. If some old coins are valuable, then <u>they are worth more than their face values</u>. Some old coins are valuable.

39

21. If <u>Mr. Keller is an engineer</u>, then Mrs. Keller is a fire fighter.
    Mrs. Keller is a fire fighter.
22. All turtles are small if <u>whales are mammals</u>.
    All turtles are small.
23. All turtles are small if <u>whales are mammals</u>.
    Not all turtles are small.
24. <u>All turtles are small</u> if whales are mammals.
    Whales are mammals.
25. If Canada is a large country, then <u>Canadians are friendly</u>.
    Canada is a large country.
26. If Mr. Wilson is wealthy, then <u>Mrs. Wilson is the president of the company</u>.
    Mr. Wilson is not wealthy.
27. If you like hamburgers, then <u>you like hot dogs</u>.
    If you like hot dogs, then <u>you like sandwiches</u>.
    You like hamburgers.
28. If <u>you like hamburgers</u>, then you like hot dogs.
    If <u>you like hot dogs</u>, then you like sandwiches.
    You don't like sandwiches.
29. Either you'll go straight home after school or you'll get into trouble.
    If you get into trouble, then <u>you'll be grounded</u>.
    You won't go straight home after school.
30. Either you'll write to me or <u>I'll write to you</u>.
    Either <u>you'll do your homework</u> or you'll flunk the course.
    You won't flunk the course and you won't write to me.
31. Either you'll be famous or <u>you'll be a bum</u>.
    Either <u>you'll be rich</u> or you'll be poor.
    You won't be poor, and you'll be famous.

Problems 32-38: Answer the question(s) asked.
32. The plumber told Mr. Welson, "If I don't fix that leak, then I won't send you a bill." The plumber worked on it for five hours but couldn't fix the leak because the plumbing was in too much of a mess and needed major repairs first. But Mr. Welson didn't want to have the major repairs done, because he was planning to sell the house soon. The plumber figured that it wasn't his fault that he didn't fix the leak, so he billed Mr. Welson for five hours of work. Did the plumber lie to Mr. Welson?
33. Diana read the ad: "If you use SUPERLASH, your eyes will be more beautiful." Diana used a different product, and her eyes were more beautiful. Did the ad lie to Diana?
34. Flora read the same ad as Diana. Flora already had beautiful eyes, and she used SUPERLASH, but her eyes didn't get any more beautiful. Did the ad lie to Flora?
35. Mr. MacIntyre read the ad: "If you want a cleaner house, then you'll use ULTRACLEAN." Mr. MacIntyre wanted a cleaner house, but he never did use ULTRACLEAN. Did the ad lie to Mr. MacIntyre?
36. Steve, a resident of Windsor, Ontario, was visiting his friend Rex, who lived in Detroit, Michigan. Steve read an ad Rex found in a newspaper: "If you're a resident of Michigan, then you're eligible to enter. Do it NOW!" Rex didn't enter the

contest, but Steve entered the contest and put his own address on the entry blank, and his entry was accepted. Did the ad lie to Steve? Did the ad lie to Rex?

37. The teacher told Emma, "If you don't do these extra credit problems, then you won't get an A this card-marking." Emma did all of the extra credit problems and did them correctly, but she still didn't get the A that card-marking. Did the teacher lie to Emma?

38. Mr. Wong told his wife, "If I stop at the store on the way home from work, I'll be about an hour late." He was about an hour late getting home from work, but he didn't stop at the store on the way. Did he lie to his wife?

TEASERS A - D: Just before the problems for this section, you were given a truth table for the sentence "P→Q." Two statements are said to be logically equivalent if and only if their truth tables are identical. Use only the letters P and Q in your answers to TEASERS A - D below. (You may also use the symbol "~" and you may use parentheses.)

  TEASER A: Find an "if-then" statement which is logically equivalent to "P→Q," but which is different from "P→Q."

  TEASER B: Find an "if-then" statement which is logically equivalent to "P or Q."

  TEASER C: Find an "or" statement and an "if-then" statement, both of which are logically equivalent to each other and to "~(P and Q)."

  TEASER D: Find an "or" statement and an "and" statement, both of which are logically equivalent to each other and to "~(P →Q)."

TEASER E: Prove that both "and' and "or" have the commutative property. That is, prove that "P and Q" is logically equivalent to "Q and P," and prove that "P or Q" is logically equivalent to "Q or P."

TEASER F: Using only the letters P, Q, and R, find an "and" sentence which is logically equivalent to the "or" sentence, "P or (Q and R)." (Hint: The symbol "~" is not used in this answer.)

TEASER G: Using only the letters P, Q, and R, find an "or" sentence which is logically equivalent to the "and" sentence, "P and (Q or R)." (Hint: The symbol "~" is not used in this answer.)

2.8 PROPOSITION, CONVERSE, INVERSE, CONTRAPOSITIVE

A **proposition** is any sentence which can take the form $P \to Q$. Once we have decided what we are going to use for the proposition, we can talk about the proposition's converse, its inverse, and its contrapositive. Although we can talk about a proposition as something which exists in its own right, a converse can exist only in relation to a proposition. That is, to talk about "converse," we must talk about the converse of some proposition. Similarly, an inverse and a contrapositive can exist only in relation to a proposition.

Definitions:
A **proposition** is a sentence which can take the form $P \to Q$.
The **converse** of the proposition $P \to Q$ is $Q \to P$.
The **inverse** of the proposition $P \to Q$ is $\sim P \to \sim Q$.
The **contrapositive** of the proposition $P \to Q$ is $\sim Q \to \sim P$.

Example 1:
Proposition: If we have rain, then we have clouds.
Converse: If we have clouds, then we have rain.
Inverse: If we don't have rain, then we don't have clouds.
Contrapositive: If we don't have clouds, then we don't have rain.
Notice that a proposition may be true without having a true converse.

Example 2:
Proposition: If you leave right now, then you'll get there on time.
Converse: If you'll get there on time, then you leave right now.
Inverse: If you don't leave right now, then you won't get there on time.
Contrapositive: If you won't get there on time, then you don't leave right now.

Example 3:
Proposition: If you won't pay attention, then you won't understand this.
Converse: If you won't understand this, then you won't pay attention.
Inverse: If you'll pay attention, then you'll understand this.
Contrapositive: If you'll understand this, then you'll pay attention.

If we know the truth value of a proposition, will that automatically tell us what the truth value is of its converse, inverse, and contrapositive? We will make a truth table to find out.

P	Q	~P	~Q	Prop $P \to Q$	Conv $Q \to P$	Inv $\sim P \to \sim Q$	Contrap $\sim Q \to \sim P$
T	T	F	F	T	T	T	T
T	F	F	T	F	T	T	F
F	T	T	F	T	F	F	T
F	F	T	T	T	T	T	T

When we look at the truth table, one of the things we see is that a proposition and its contrapositive are equivalent statements. That is, given that we know the truth value of the proposition, then its contrapositive has to have the same truth value. So we will make

Statement 1: A proposition and its contrapositive always have the same truth value.

Looking at the truth table again, we see that the converse and inverse of a proposition are equivalent statements. Neither one is equivalent to the proposition, but they are equivalent to each other.

Statement 2: The converse and inverse of a proposition always have the same truth value as each other, but the proposition may have a different truth value than this.

Now we look at the table and compare the truth values of a proposition and its converse. We see that a proposition and its converse are NOT equivalent statements.

Statement 3: A proposition and its converse do not have to have the same truth value.

We may combine Statements 1-3 above and get a

Summary of Truth Values:
1. A proposition and its contrapositive are equivalent statements—that is, they have the same truth value.
2. A proposition and its converse are NOT equivalent statements.
3. The converse and inverse of a proposition are equivalent statements.

CLASS DISCUSSION PROBLEMS

1. Dje-Han asked his brother, "This sentence says, 'If I can't get the car, then I won't go.' Is that the inverse?" Dje-Da answered, "First you have to tell me what the proposition is. There's no such thing as just 'the inverse.'" Dje-Han said, "We're studying inverses in this section, so there must be such a thing."
   Who is right? Support your answer.
2. What do we mean when we say that two statements are equivalent statements?

Problems 3-7: Each problem makes a statement in symbolized form. Using this statement as the proposition, give the converse, the inverse, and the contrapositive of the proposition.

Example:
Problem: $P \rightarrow Q$
Answer: converse, $Q \rightarrow P$; inverse, $\sim P \rightarrow \sim Q$; contrapositive, $\sim Q \rightarrow \sim P$

3. $Q \rightarrow P$
4. $\sim R \rightarrow X$
5. $A \rightarrow \sim B$
6. $(A \text{ or } B) \rightarrow Q$
7. $\sim T \rightarrow \sim S$

43

Problems 8-13: Each problem gives either the converse, the inverse, or the contrapositive of a proposition. You are to state the proposition and the other two kinds of statements which are missing.

Example:
  Problem: Q→P is the converse of the proposition.
  Answer: proposition, P→Q; inverse, ~P→~Q; contrapositive, ~Q→~P

8. R→S is the converse of the proposition.
9. R→S is the inverse of the proposition.
10. R→S is the contrapositive of the proposition.
11. ~T→U is the converse of the proposition.
12. ~A→~B is the inverse of the proposition.
13. F→~G is the contrapositive of the proposition.

Problems 14-16: In each problem, a statement is followed by some lettered statements. Accept each first statement as a proposition, and tell the relation (converse, inverse, contrapositive, proposition, none) of the lettered statement to the first statement. (Hint: Try symbolizing the statements in order to help yourself decide.)

Example:
  Problem: If this is Sunday, then I'll eat my hat.
              a.   If this isn't Sunday, then I won't eat my hat.
              b.   If this isn't Sunday, then I'll eat my hat.
  Answer: a.   inverse
              b.   none

14. If this is Monday, then you're crazy.
    a.   If you're crazy, then this is Monday.
    b.   If this isn't Monday, then you're not crazy.
    c.   If it's false that this isn't Monday, then you're crazy.
    d.   If you're not crazy, then this is Monday.
    e.   If you're not crazy, then this isn't Monday.
15. If you want fantastic results, then you'll use SUPERGREAT.
    a.   If you won't use SUPERGREAT, then you don't want fantastic results.
    b.   If you don't want fantastic results, then you won't use SUPERGREAT.
    c.   If you'll use SUPERGREAT, then you want fantastic results.
    d.   If it's false that you want fantastic results, then you'll use SUPERGREAT.
16. If you don't learn this, then you're not trying hard enough.
    a.   If you learn this, then you're trying hard enough.
    b.   If it's false that you learn this, then it's false that you're trying hard enough.
    c.   If you're trying hard enough, then you learn this.
    d.   If you're not trying hard enough, then you don't learn this.

Problems 17-25: For each problem, two statements are given. Tell whether or not the two statements are equivalent statements, and support your answer.

17. P→Q; ~Q→~P
18. A→B; B→A
19. R→S; ~R→~S
20. T→U; ~~T→U
21. ~G→H; G→~H
22. A or ~B; ~B or A
23. X and ~Y; ~Y and ~~X
24. (P or Q)→R; ~R→~(P or Q).
25. (P and Q)→(R and S); (R and S)→(P and Q).

Problems 26-29: Use the "Summary of Truth Values" which is given just before these problems, but do <u>not</u> use your knowledge of the world otherwise. In each problem, a statement is followed by lettered statements, and you are told the truth value of the first statement ("T" or "F"). Using this truth value and the "Summary of Truth Values," tell the truth value ("T," "F," or "?") of each lettered statement. Be prepared to explain your answers.

Example:
Problem: If this is Sunday, then I'll eat my hat. (T)
   a. If this isn't Sunday, then I won't eat my hat.
   b. If I won't eat my hat, then this isn't Sunday.
Answer: a. ?
          b. T
Explanation: Statement "a" is the inverse of the given statement. Since the given statement is true, items 2 and 3 of the "Summary" say we don't know the truth value of statement "a." Statement "b" is the contrapositive of the given statement. Again, the given statement is true, so (from item 1 of the "Summary") statement "b" is true.

26. If you wear nice clothes to school, then your teachers will be impressed. (T)
   a. If your teachers will be impressed, then you wear nice clothes to school.
   b. If your teachers won't be impressed, then you don't wear nice clothes to school.
   c. If you don't wear nice clothes to school, then your teachers won't be impressed.
27. Same as problem 26, except assume that the first statement is false.
28. If your forehead is tattooed, then your parents didn't object. (T)
   a. If it's false that your forehead is tattooed, then your parents objected.
   b. If it's false that your forehead isn't tattooed, then it's false that your parents objected.
   c. If your parents objected, then your forehead isn't tattooed.
   d. If your parents didn't object, then your forehead is tattooed.

45

29. If you are bilingual, then you speak two languages. (T)
    a. If you speak two languages, then you are bilingual.
    b. If you aren't bilingual, then you don't speak two languages.
    c. If you don't speak two languages, then you are not bilingual.

2.9 SUBSTITUTION OF CONVERSE OR INVERSE FOR ITS PROPOSITION

Given that a proposition is true, we know from the preceding section that its converse and its inverse may be either true or false. But one of the most common mistakes in reasoning is the substitution of the converse or the inverse of a proposition for the proposition. That is, given a true statement, many people will use the converse (or the inverse) of the statement and think that it must be true because the statement is true.

Example 1:

Mr. Wong told his wife, "If I stop at the store on the way home from work, I'll be about an hour late." That afternoon, Mrs. Wong realized that her husband was 55 minutes overdue from work, and she thought, "He must have stopped at the store on his way home."

We see that Mrs. Wong was thinking, "If he's about an hour late, he stopped at the store on the way home from work." She has substituted the converse of the proposition for the proposition.

Example 2:

The teacher told Emma, "If you don't do these extra credit problems, then you won't get an A this card-marking." Emma did all of the extra credit problems because she wanted an A, and she was sure the teacher had promised her an A if she did the problems.

We see here that Emma was thinking, "If I do the extra credit problems, then I'll get an A this card-marking." Emma has substituted the inverse of the proposition for the proposition.

CLASS DISCUSSION PROBLEMS

1. This section says it is faulty reasoning if we substitute the converse or the inverse of a proposition for the proposition. Is it also faulty reasoning if we substitute the contrapositive of a proposition for the proposition? Support your answer.
2. Suppose we know that two statements of different forms (for example, an "or" statement and an "if-then" statement) happen to be equivalent statements. Is it faulty reasoning if we substitute one for the other? Support your answer.

Problems 3-7: Tell whether or not the person in the problem was guilty of faulty reasoning. If he was, then tell what was wrong with his reasoning.

3. Mr. Connwell read the ad: "If your lawn will look better, then you'll use FERTILIZO." He wanted a better-looking lawn, so he used FERTILIZO, but his lawn looked the same as it always had. He thought the Federal Trade Commission should do something about the false advertising by the makers of FERTILIZO.

4. Antonio saw the sign in the pizzeria: "If you're going to get the biggest pizza in town, then you're going to order our SUPERWHOPPER pizza." Antonio loved pizza, so he went in and ordered the SUPERWHOPPER pizza. When he got the pizza, however, it was only 15 cm in diameter. Antonio was angry, and he complained to the manager about the misleading sign in the window.

5. Doreen had a date that night, but her mother told her, "If you don't apologize to your brother for the way you treated him, then you're not going out tonight." Doreen didn't want to break her date, so she apologized to her brother for the way she treated him, but her mother still made her stay home. Doreen told her mother that they'd made a bargain and that Doreen had kept her end of it but her mother had broken the bargain.

6. Mr. Chu had lived under communist rule in China but had managed to escape to the United States. He knew that a communist ruler always made sure that the country had socialized medicine, so when he heard that the U.S. President was in favor of socialized medicine, he was sure that the President was a communist.

7. Mrs. Smother read the ad: "If you don't try our product, then you'll be sorry." She didn't want to be sorry, so she tried the product. She didn't like the product, however, and she was sorry she'd tried it. She wrote to the president of the company and complained that the advertising for the product was misleading.

2.10 "ONLY IF" SENTENCES AND THEIR TRUTH VALUES

An "only if" sentence is a sentence of the form "P only if Q." Following are some examples of "only if" sentences.

1. I'll do my homework tonight only if you explain it again first.
2. I'll go hiking tomorrow only if I feel better by then.
3. You are eligible for this contest only if you're a resident of Illinois.
4. You can see an invisible tiger only if you have unusually good eyesight.
5. You can go on your date tonight only if you apologize to your brother first.

47

Now let's think about the sentence, "P only if Q." If you emphasize the words "only if" as you read it, you'll see that it is saying, "The <u>only</u> way we'll have P is to have Q." In other words, Q is a necessary condition for P. But you learned in section 2.5 that this is another way of saying "P → Q." So "P only if Q" is the same as "P→Q."

We will list the conclusions of section 2.5 again and also add what we've found out since then:

The following are equivalent statements:
1. P only if Q.
2. If P, then Q.
3. Q if P.
4. P→Q
5. ~ Q→ ~ P
6. P is a sufficient condition for Q.
7. Q is a necessary condition for P.

CLASS DISCUSSION PROBLEMS

1. Is there a TV set in your home? Is there only a TV set in your home?
2. Are there two sides in a triangle? Are there only two sides in a triangle?
3. Does a square have two sides? Does it have only two sides?
4. In general, does a rose have one petal? Does it have only one petal?
5. Would you like to have some pizza right now? Would you like to have only some pizza right now?

Problems 6-10: Go back to the five examples in this section.
6. Put Example 1 in "if-then" form.
7. Put Example 2 in "if-then" form.
8. Put Example 3 in "if-then" form.
9. Put Example 4 in "if-then" form.
10. Put Example 5 in "if-then" form.

Problems 11-16: Go back to the examples in section 2.6.
11. Put Example 1 in "only if" form.
12. Put Example 3 in "only if" form.
13. Put Example 4 in "only if" form.
14. Put Example 5 in "only if" form.
15. Put Example 7 in "only if" form.
16. Put Example 8 in "only if" form.

17. The contest advertisement stated, "You are eligible for this contest only if you're a resident of Kentucky."
   a. Roberto was a resident of Wyoming, but he entered the contest anyhow, and his entry was accepted. Did the ad lie to Roberto?
   b. Chi-Hai was a resident of Kentucky, but he was visiting Taipei for three months when he read the ad. He sent in his entry from Taipei and his entry was accepted. Did the ad lie to Chi-Hai?

48

c. Cleo was a resident of Kentucky. She sent in her entry, but it was rejected. Did the ad lie to Cleo?

18. Brett's father told him, "You can use the car tonight only if you wash it first." Brett washed the car but his father still wouldn't let him use it. Brett was angry and he said his father lied to him, but his father said he didn't lie. Who was right? Support your answer.

19. Flora had a lovely voice, and Mr. Rowly, the vocal music teacher, kept asking Flora to drop her study hall and sign up for the choir. Flora finally told him, "I'll drop my study hall and sign up for the choir next Tuesday only if you don't bug me about it any more in the meantime." Mr. Rowly agreed not to say anything more to her about it in the meantime. Well, the following Tuesday came and went, and Flora had not even tried to drop her study hall and sign up for the choir. Mr. Rowly told Flora that she broke her word, and Flora said she didn't. Who was right? Support your answer.

20. Karen had wealthy parents and a brother that no girl wanted to date. Karen asked her best friend, Ann, why no one would date her brother. Ann told her, "When he talks, most of the time it sounds like he doesn't know what he's talking about and is just trying to impress the girl. And he's as likely as not to be crabby for no reason, and you know what he's like when he's crabby." Karen said, "Ann, why don't you have a date with him? Do it as a favor to me, will you?" Ann answered "Karen I think you're great, but I won't go out with your brother." Karen kept after Ann about it, and finally Ann said, "Look, Karen. I'll date your brother only if you pay me $1,000 for it." Ann thought that the matter would be ended. But the next day, Karen handed her $1,000 and said, "Now you have to date my brother once." Ann protested that she hadn't agreed to date him for $1,000, and she gave the money back. Karen said that it didn't matter whether or not Ann kept the money. She said that Ann had agreed to date her brother if she paid Ann $1,000 for it, and she had paid Ann $1,000 for it. Who was right? Support your answer.

21. Barry, Hisashi, and Fernandel all read the ad which said, "You'll like this product only if you're hard to please. Your money back if this ad hasn't told you the truth."
a. Barry was hard to please. He tried the product but didn't like it, so he wanted his money back. Was he entitled to a refund? Why?
b. Hisashi wasn't hard to please. He tried the product and didn't like it. Was he entitled to a refund? Why?
c. Fernandel wasn't hard to please. He tried the product and liked it. Was he entitled to a refund? Why?

22. Harriet's mother was going to visit some relatives for the weekend and wanted Harriet to go with her. Harriet didn't want to go, and she tried to talk her mother into letting her stay home alone. Her mother said, "I've had about enough of this nonsense from you! The only way you're not going with me is if you can talk your grandmother into letting you stay with her." Harriet thought that staying with her grandmother was a lot better than going to visit those other relatives, so

2.11 ARGUMENTS, PREMISES, AND CONCLUSIONS

An **argument** is a series of statements meeting these conditions:
1. One of the statements is supposed to be based on, or supported by, the others. This statement is called a **conclusion.**
2. The other statements (that is, the statements which are not a conclusion) are called **premises.**

Example 1:

Premise: All flowers are pretty.

Premise: A rose is a flower.

Conclusion: So a rose must be pretty.

Example 2:

Premise: A rhinoceros is an animal.

Premise: No animal is a vegetable.

Conclusion: Therefore, a rhinoceros is not a vegetable.

In everyday speaking, we do not usually use short sentences like the sentences in the examples above. Our spoken arguments are more likely to sound like the examples which follow.

Example 3:

Abe is talking to Dolly, a blind girl.

Abe: "All flowers are pretty."

Dolly: "A rose is a flower, so it must be pretty."

We see that Dolly's argument is the same argument as in Example 1. Here, the first premise is Abe's statement, and the second premise is the first part of Dolly's statement. The conclusion is the last part of Dolly's statement (starting with the word "so").

Example 4:

Abe: "A rhinoceros is an animal."

Dolly: "Then a rhinoceros can't be a vegetable, because no animal is a vegetable."

Dolly's argument here is the same argument as in Example 2. In this case, the first premise is Abe's statement. The second premise is the last part of Dolly's statement (notice the word "because"), and the conclusion is the first part of Dolly's statement (notice the word "then").[1]

Example 5:

Francis: "A rose must be pretty, because all flowers are pretty and a rose is a flower."

---

[1] In general, words or phrases such as "because," "for," "since," "if," "when," and "in view of the fact that" will indicate that what is said next is a <u>premise</u>. Words or phrases such as "therefore," "so," "then," "hence," "thus," "consequently," and "it follows that" will indicate that what is said next is a <u>conclusion</u>.

In this argument, the conclusion is first, and the premises are last (starting with "because").

Any argument can be put in the form of an "if-then" sentence. The premises are the "if" part, and the conclusion is the "then" part.

Example 6:

If all flowers are pretty and a rose is a flower, then a rose is pretty.

Example 7:

A rose is pretty, if all flowers are pretty and a rose is a flower.

Example 8:

If all flowers are pretty and if a rose is a flower, then a rose is pretty.

Example 9:

If a rhinoceros is an animal, and if no animal is a vegetable, then a rhinoceros is not a vegetable.

In all of the examples above, the conclusions were logical. But we know that not everyone thinks logically, so some arguments may have illogical conclusions.

Example 10:

Fran: "Most birds can fly, and a robin is a bird, so a robin must be able to fly."

The conclusion here is not logical. The first premise says that <u>most</u> birds can fly, which leaves room for exceptions. The second premise does not state whether or not a robin is one of the exceptions to the first premise, so the conclusion does not follow from the premises. In other words, a logical thinker could believe the premises and yet not believe the conclusion.

Example 11:

Paul: "All triangles have three sides, so a zebra must have stripes."

Here, too, the conclusion is not logical. In this case, the conclusion has nothing to do with the premise.

Summary:
1. The definitions of argument, premise, and conclusion are given at the beginning of this section.
2. Any argument is an "if-then" sentence, where the premises are the "if" part and the conclusion is the "then" part.
3. A conclusion may or may not be logical.

CLASS DISCUSSION PROBLEMS

Problems 1-7: Each problem is an argument. State each argument as an "if-then" sentence.
1. All human beings are mortal. Yvette is a human being. So Yvette is mortal.
2. All lilacs are pretty. All lilacs are flowers. Then all flowers are pretty.
3. All lilacs are pretty. All lilacs are flowers. Thus, some flowers are pretty.

51

4. If Mrs. Hernandez is an attorney, then she is a college graduate. Mrs. Hernandez is an attorney. Therefore, Mrs. Hernandez is a college graduate. (Hint: The first premise is of the form "P → Q," which can be written as, "P implies Q.")

5. Roses are red. Violets are blue. Hence, sugar is sweet, and I love you.

6. Mrs. Rosa doesn't like cats, and no housewife likes cats. Consequently, Mrs. Rosa is a housewife.

7. My dog doesn't like cats, and no mouse likes cats. So my dog is a mouse.

8. You may have noticed in problems 1-7 above that some of the conclusions seemed logical and some did not. State which conclusions appear to you to be
   a. logical.
   b. illogical.

Problems 9-15: Each problem can be made into an argument. Tell which parts are the premises and which part is the conclusion of the argument.

Example:
  Problem: A rose must be pretty (1), because all flowers are pretty (2) and a rose is a flower (3).
  Answer: The premises are (2) and (3), and the conclusion is (1).

9. José must really be smart (1), because he gets all A's (2) and he takes hard classes (3).

10. I know you're wrong (1), because my brother said so (2).

11. If an eight-footed elephant exists, then it must have wings. (1) But anything which has wings can fly. (2) So if an eight-footed elephant exists, then it can fly. (3)

12. Miss Downey told me that's right (1), so I know it's right (2), because Miss Downey never lies (3).

13. A crow is black (1) and a raven is black (2). Then all birds must be black (3), since both crows and ravens are birds (4).

14. If you believe that (1), then you must be pretty dumb (2), because that's obviously false (3).

15. Miss Blonding is too good a teacher to give us a test when we're not ready for it (1), and we're not ready for a test on this (2), so Miss Blonding won't give us a test on it yet (3).

16. In an argument,
    a. what is the least number of premises there may be?
    b. do all of the premises have to be true?
    c. does the conclusion have to be true?
    d. does the conclusion have to be logical?

17. Is it possible to have a logical conclusion in an argument if the conclusion is false? Support your answer.

2.12 CLASS DISCUSSION
PROBLEMS AND QUESTIONS
FOR CHAPTER REVIEW

1. a. What is the meaning of the symbol "→"?
   b. Give an example of the correct use of this symbol.
2. a. What is the meaning of the symbol "~"?
   b. Let D = Dorothy will go to the ball game tonight.
      (1) What is the meaning of " ~ D"?
      (2) What is the meaning of " ~~ D"?
3. Let D = Dorothy will not go to the ball game tonight. What is the meaning of "~D"?
4. a. If you know that a sentence of the form "P or Q" is true, what (if anything) do you know about the truth values of P and of Q?
   b. Referring to the first tattoo on your forehead if necessary, complete this sentence: "The sentence 'P or Q' is false if and only if_____."
   c. Suppose someone tells you something of the form "P or Q," and suppose you know the person told the truth and you also know that P is true. What (if anything) do you know about the truth value of Q?
5. Jake believes the statement, "The Surgeon General has determined that cigarette smoking is dangerous to your health." He also believes that the Surgeon General has never made a mistake in matters of health. If Jake is a very logical person, what will be his conclusion about this?
6. Suppose someone says to you, "Either you're crazy or I'm crazy," and you know that you're not crazy. What logical conclusion follows from this?
7. a. If you know that the sentence "P and Q" is false, what (if anything) do you know about the truth values of P and of Q?
   b. Referring to the second tattoo on your forehead if necessary, complete this sentence: "The sentence 'P and Q' is true if and only if_____."
8. Let N = Noelle will go. Let S = Scott will go.
   a. What is the meaning of " ~ N or ~ S"?
   b. What is the meaning of " ~(N or S)"?
   c. What is the meaning of " ~ N and ~ S"?
   d. What is the meaning of " ~(N and S)"?
   e. What's the difference in meanings between your "a" and "d" answers?
   f. What's the difference in meanings between your "b" and "c" answers?
9. State each sentence in simpler form. If the sentence can't be simplified, then answer "simplified."
   a. It's false that Terri doesn't like tennis.
   b. It's false that Terri dislikes tennis.
   c. It isn't true that it's false that Zachariah told me you were good-looking.
   d. It isn't the case that you don't care.

10. You are given that the sentence "A → B" is true. State the truth value ("T" or "F") of each of the following sentences. (Answer "F" if the statement is not necessarily true.)
    a. A is a necessary condition for B.
    b. A is a sufficient condition for B.
    c. B is a necessary condition for A.
    d. B is a sufficient condition for A.
    e. A is neither a sufficient nor a necessary condition for B.
    f. A is both a sufficient and a necessary condition for B.
    g. B is neither a sufficient nor a necessary condition for A.
    h. B is both a sufficient and a necessary condition for A.

11. Otto said, "If I don't get an A on this test, I'm going to quit trying." Ned replied, "That may be enough to make you quit, but it isn't enough for me." If both boys are telling the truth, which of the following conclusions are implied?
    a. Ned thinks it takes more to make him quit than it takes to make Otto quit.
    b. It doesn't take much to make Otto quit trying.
    c. It takes a lot to make Ned quit trying.
    d. Otto's statement is true for him, but it's false for Ned.

12. Complete the sentence, "An 'if-then' sentence is false if and only if _____."

13. Using your knowledge of the world, state the truth value ("T," "F," or "?") of each sentence.
    a. You dislike apple pie if you're over 100 years old.
    b. You like apple pie if you're over 100 years old.
    c. If you don't have eight legs, then you're not an octopus.
    d. If you don't have eight legs, then you're a spider.
    e. If you have brown hair, then you have brown eyes.
    f. An egg has feathers only if a dog is an animal.

14. Accept each sentence as true. If a logical conclusion follows, then state the conclusion; otherwise, answer "CNN" (conclusion not necessary).
    a. If you travel a lot, then you know what I mean. You travel a lot.
    b. If you travel a lot, then you know what I mean. You don't travel a lot.
    c. If a figure is a triangle, then it has three sides. This figure is a triangle.
    d. If a figure is a triangle, then it has three sides. This figure isn't a triangle.
    e. If a figure is a triangle, then it has three sides. This figure has three sides.
    f. If a figure is a triangle, then it has three sides. This figure doesn't have three sides.
    g. Your hands are blue with pink polka dots only if you are cold now. You are cold now.
    h. Your hands are blue with pink polka dots only if you are cold now. Your hands aren't blue with pink polka dots.

15. The queen told her beautiful victim, "I'll spare you only if you promise to marry my ugly son." The victim promised to marry the queen's ugly son, and the queen promptly killed her. Did the queen lie? Support your answer.

16. Suppose someone has a wrong answer for problem 15. What is probably wrong with that person's reasoning?

17. In problem 15, suppose the queen's statement is the truth, and suppose she killed her victim. Did the victim promise to marry the queen's ugly son? Support your answer.

18. If someone has a wrong answer for problem 17, what is propably wrong with that person's reasoning?

19. The ad said, "We can guarantee your satisfaction only if you send us your order before midnight tonight." Roosevelt sent in his order before midnight that same night. Has he been promised that they <u>will</u> guarantee his satisfaction? Has he been promised that they <u>can</u> guarantee his satisfaction?

20. a. Does an argument always have at least one premise?
    b. Does an argument always have at least one conclusion?
    c. What is the greatest number of premises an argument may have?
    d. What is the greatest number of conclusions an argument may have?

Problems 21-24: Each problem is an argument.
   a. Tell which parts are the premises and which parts are the conclusions.
   b. Tell whether or not the conclusions are logical.

21. If it rains too much, then the plants will not grow well. (1) The plants will not grow well. (2) So it rains too much. (3)

22. Pearl and Nora are fighting again (1), and whenever they fight, they end up crying (2). So Pearl and Nora will end up crying. (3)

23. I think that what Mr. Wronkewitz said must be true (1), because he's never lied to me about anything else (2).

24. Walter likes Canada (1), because Canada is a beautiful country (2) and Walter likes beautiful countries (3).

CHAPTER 3

SOME BASIC CONCEPTS FOR CRITICAL THINKING

3.1 WHAT'S THE DIFFERENCE BETWEEN ''PROBABLE'' AND ''POSSIBLE''?

3.2 ALLEGORIES, OLD SAYINGS, AND LITERARY REFERENCES

3.3 PEOPLE MAY HAVE DIFFERENT <u>FEELINGS</u> ABOUT THE SAME WORD

3.4 A CHANGED DEFINITION MAY PRODUCE A CHANGED CONCLUSION

3.5 DON'T JUMP TO A CONCLUSION — THE OBVIOUS ONE MAY BE WRONG

3.6 EYEWITNESSES AND CIRCUMSTANTIAL EVIDENCE

3.7 IMPLICATIONS AND INFERENCES

3.8 CLASS DISCUSSION PROBLEMS AND QUESTIONS FOR CHAPTER REVIEW

3.1 WHAT'S THE DIFFERENCE BETWEEN "PROBABLE" AND "POSSIBLE"?

An event is **probable** if it is more likely to happen than not. An event is **possible** if there is any chance at all that it will happen.

Example 1:

It is possible that you'll live to be 110 years old, but it is probable that you won't.

Example 2:

It is possible that you'll live to be 110 years old, but it is not probable that you will.

Example 3:

It's possible that if you toss an honest coin 100 times, you'll get "heads" every time. But it's probable that you'll get "heads" only 40-60 times.

"Maybe" is another word used in place of "it is possible that." (Or we might say, "It may be," instead of, "It is possible.")

Example 4:

Eliza's parents want her to stay home on school nights. This is a school night, and a friend has asked Eliza to go somewhere. Eliza says, "Well, maybe my parents will let me go, but they probably won't."

Example 5:

When you toss an honest coin 100 times, maybe you'll get 100 "heads" in a row, but it's improbable.

Example 6:

You may get away with pulling a practical joke on him, but he'll probably find out that you're the one who did it.

CLASS DISCUSSION PROBLEMS

1. If something is possible, <u>must</u> it also be probable?
2. If something is probable, <u>must</u> it also be possible?
3. We know that if we toss an honest coin, then there are exactly as many chances for "heads" as for "tails" to turn up when the coin lands. If we toss such a coin,
    a. is it possible that "heads" will turn up?
    b. is it possible that "heads" will not turn up?
    c. is it probable that "heads" will turn up?
    d. is it probable that "heads" will not turn up?
4. Read what happened, and then tell whether or not Jeff's sentence is OK. If his sentence is not OK, then tell what's wrong with it.
    Jeff was thinking about the truth value of a statement he read. He didn't have enough information to decide whether or not the statement was true. Jeff said, "Well, going by the information I have about it,
    a. maybe it's true and maybe it isn't."
    b. it's possible and it's not possible."
    c. possibly it's true, but possibly it's false."
    d. it may be true, but it may be false."

5. If you say that something is not probable, are you also saying that
   a. it is not possible?
   b. it is possible?
6. If you say that something is not possible, are you also saying that it is not probable?
7. Which is the stronger statement—"It is possible," or "It is probable"?

Problems 8-13: Accept the given information as true. Replace each blank with "possible," "not possible," or "probable," whichever seems to make the statement the most accurate.

8. Joshua's parents are very devout in their religion, which forbids marriage between someone of their faith and someone not of their faith. It is _____ that Joshua's parents will not approve of his dating a girl who is not of their faith.
9. Mr. Rishland insists that his house be kept clean. If he sees his teenagers track in mud from outside and they don't make an effort to clean it up, it is _____ that Mr. Rishland will speak to them about it.
10. Mrs. Lapetin bought three BRAND X cars, and all three were lemons. She decided that all BRAND X cars must be lemons. It is _____ that Mrs. Lapetin was right.
11. If you ask five different people to choose a number at random, it is _____ that all five people will choose the same number.
12. If you flip a coin which has "heads" on each side, then it is _____ that the coin will turn up "tails."
13. Mrs. Honsam is 75 years old and is loved by everyone in her neighborhood. If her neighbors find out that someone has robbed Mrs. Honsam, it is _____ that they will not be indifferent about it.

3.2 ALLEGORIES, OLD SAYINGS, AND LITERARY REFERENCES

An **allegory** is a disguised statement about human beings. In Aesop's fables, we find allegories in the form of stories. In some old sayings, we find allegories in the form of simple statements. In the Bible, we find allegories both in the form of simple statements and in the form of parables.

You may wonder what this has to do with critical thinking. The answer to this is in two parts: first, learn to recognize an allegory for what it is—that is, learn to take its intended meaning rather than its literal meaning; second, many people use allegories and make literary references when they talk, and you cannot think critically about what they say unless you understand what they are saying.

Example 1:

Nerissa: "That new boy is really an Adonis, isn't he?"

Adonis was a handsome youth in Greek mythology. If you did not have some idea that Nerissa was using "an Adonis" in place of "handsome," you wouldn't know what she said.

Example 2:

Lynne: "My sister says she's glad she's not pretty, because other people always try to find fault with good-looking girls. But I think that's just sour grapes."

If you don't know what Lynne means by "sour grapes," her last sentence probably doesn't make sense to you. "Sour grapes" refers to finding fault with something which we know we can't have. It comes from one of Aesop's fables, "The Fox and the Grapes." The story goes like this:

A fox saw a grapevine, and at the top of the vine was the most beautiful bunch of grapes he had ever seen. He could imagine how delicious they would be, so he tried to reach them but could not. He tried again and again but no matter how hard he tried he couldn't reach those grapes. He finally said, "I don't want them. They're probably sour, anyhow."

Example 3:

Terry (an all-A student): "My brother was born with a lot of brain damage, and my parents want me to teach him everything I learn in school. They just won't admit that you can't make a silk purse out of a sow's ear."

Terry is not suggesting here that comparing him with his brother is like comparing a silk purse to a sow's ear. He is saying that his brother cannot learn everything a normal boy learns.

CLASS DISCUSSION PROBLEMS

Problems 1-4: A statement is made and is followed by several lettered statements. Assume that the first statement is not to be taken literally.

    A.   Choose the lettered statements which are implied by the first statement.

    B.   Tell why you did not choose the other statements.

Example:

Problem: You can't make a silk purse out of a sow's ear.

    a.   Silk doesn't come from the ear of a pig.

    b.   It's no use trying to be good at something when you don't have the ability for it.

    c.   It's no use trying to learn something well if it's hard for you to understand.

Answer: A. b

              B. Answer "a" is wrong because that's the literal meaning of the given statement. Answer "c" is wrong because the given statement talks about making something out of something else which can't be changed into it, but in "c" it's possible that something is hard to understand now but you'll understand it easily later.

60

Comment: Answer "b" would also be wrong if the word "ability" were changed to "training."

1. A stitch in time saves nine.
   a. If your clothing has a little tear in it, you'll save a lot of sewing if you mend it now instead of waiting until later.
   b. If someone does something you don't like, you should let him know. Otherwise, he may keep doing it until you finally explode about it.
   c. If you find that you are starting to fall behind in your studies, you'd better start catching up right away instead of waiting until later.
   d. It is easier to break a bad habit as soon as it is discovered than it is to break it after it has been with you for several years.

2. The grass always looks greener on the other side of the fence.
   a. You may envy the life someone else leads, but you might not be any happier leading his life than you are right now.
   b. Whenever there is a fence between two plots of grass, the light plays tricks, making the grass on the other side of the fence look greener.
   c. You may think that someone has an easier life than yours when his life is really harder than yours.

3. It is better to light one small candle than to curse the darkness.
   a. Cursing is wrong.
   b. If you go into a dark room, it's better to try to find a match or a light switch than to stand there complaining about the darkness.
   c. If you find a lot of ignorant people, it's better to try to teach one of them something than to complain about the ignorance of everyone.
   d. If you find out something about a subject in which not many answers are known, you should share your discovery with others instead of complaining that the other things you want to know have not yet been discovered.

4. It's no use crying over spilled milk.
   a. If milk has spilled, then your crying about it isn't going to put it back into the glass.
   b. If something has happened to make you unhappy, your tears will not undo the fact that it happened.
   c. You can't change what has already happened by crying about it.

Problems 5-13: Choosing from statements "a" through "h" below, replace each blank by the letter of the statement most appropriate to the situation.
   a. The grass always looks greener on the other side of the fence.
   b. You can't teach an old dog new tricks.
   c. Where there's smoke, there's fire.
   d. It's no use crying over spilled milk.
   e. You shouldn't judge another person until you've walked in his shoes for two weeks.

f. That's just sour grapes.

g. A bird in the hand is worth two in the bush.

h. One bad apple will spoil a barrelful.

5. Mr. Uhrlance, a mining engineer, had been at his job for many years and knew his job well. He was known for being set in his ways. Ms. Vincenzia, a recently graduated mining engineer who was his assistant, showed him a new instrument which instantaneously showed the composition of any mineral within an accuracy of 1/1000th of 1%. Mr. Uhrlance told her, "No, don't bother to show me how to work it. I won't use it. I don't trust these new inventions. I'll just stick with my old ways." Ms. Vincenzia thought, "Well, I guess the old saying must be true: _____ ."

6. Doreen said to Thais, "If I were the boss, I wouldn't be crabby all the time like Ms. Youngel is with us. We do our work, and she could act pleased with us once in a while, but she never does. She acts like a slave driver, and she has no reason to act like that." Thais said, "You don't know whether she has a reason or not; _____ ."

7. Mr. Innels: "I heard that the Muirlands go out and stay out 'til all hours of the night and come home drunk two or three times a week."
Mrs. Innels: "That's not true. Neither one of them ever drinks. Their religion forbids it."
Mr. Innels: "Well, there must be something to the story. After all, _____ ."

8. Norman had been offered a good job and had to let the people know within a week whether or not he would accept the job. If he accepted, he would sign a one-year contract. But he had applied for an even better job and might not know whether or not he would be the one hired for it until four days after the first job offer expired. He talked to a friend about it, trying to decide what to do. His friend said, "I think you should wait until the last day they gave you to accept the first job, and if you don't hear anything from the other people, then take the first job. _____ ."

9. An excellent female role was being cast for a movie, and a famous Hollywood actress was thought to be a sure thing for the part. However, the role was given to someone else. Someone asked the famous actress later why she didn't get the part, and she answered, "Oh, I didn't want that part. It will take too many months to shoot the film, and I don't want to be tied up that long." Someone else overheard her and said, "I don't believe that. I think _____ ."

10. Oliver's parents were buying a new bicycle for his older sister, and Oliver asked why he couldn't have one, too. His parents told him that they couldn't afford two bicycles now but that they'd get one for him, too, when he was his sister's age. Oliver said, "I don't want one, anyhow. You'd probably yell at me if I got mud on the tires or a scratch on a fender or something." His mother said to his father, " _____ _____ ."

11. Mr. Kinler, a registered nurse, said, "I have to put up with unreasonable demands from patients and from doctors, and I work around sick people all the time, and I have to work different shifts. I should have gone into teaching. Teachers have to be at school only about 7½ hours a day, and 45 minutes of that is for lunch. They get an hour a day that they don't have to be teaching, and they get extra time off at Thanksgiving, Christmas, and Easter, and they get all summer off besides. Yes, I think teaching is a much better job than nursing." His wife answered, "You might not think so if you were a teacher— _____."

12. Verda told her father about a student in one of her classes who seemed always to be trying to cause trouble for the teacher. Her father said, "If I were your teacher, I'd throw him out before his troublemaking started spreading to the other students. _____."

13. Mr. Offnar, a tax accountant, had just discovered an error he'd made in a client's tax return. The tax return had been filed some years before that, and it was too late now to file an amended return and get a refund. Mr. Offnar was honest about it and told his client, and he paid his client out of his own pocket the same amount the refund would have been if the error had been discovered in time. Mr. Offnar was unhappy about the error, for he thought that it would decrease his client's confidence in him. His partner said to him. "There's nothing you can do about it now, and _____, so cheer up. You won't make that same mistake again."

14. What's the difference between saying, "He's as mad as a hatter," and saying, "He's as mad as a wet hen"?

15. a. What is meant by the statement, "The end justifies the means"?[1]

    b. Do you agree with this statement? Why?

16. You may have heard the statement, "One should always do his best." Do you agree with this old saying? Why?

3.3 PEOPLE MAY HAVE DIFFERENT FEELINGS ABOUT THE SAME WORD

Two people may agree on the meaning of a word and yet have different feelings about the word. For example, suppose someone mentions the word "travel." The experience people have had with travel is likely to color their feelings about travel.

---

[1] In this case, the word "means" means "ways used to get an end result."

Example 1:

Sandy's father is in the Air Force, and the family has moved many times because Sandy's father gets transferred to different bases. To Sandy, "travel" means that she has to leave her friends and her school. She wishes she could stay in one place and not have to keep moving all the time.

Example 2:

Ms. Norsten has always been tied down with family responsibilities, but she has read many travel folders. She thinks, "It would be so wonderful to be free to travel to some of these lovely places I've read about!"

Example 3:

Mr. and Mrs. Richbucks like to impress their friends by talking about the places they've been. They think, "Where can we go that's different, a place our friends haven't gone yet?"

Example 4:

Mr. and Mrs. Walday have four young children. When they think of traveling, they think of all the problems of taking four young children along. There are just too many problems, so they stay home.

Example 5:

Patty has lived in one place all of her life. Her father and mother both work, and she goes to school. She thinks the family is in a rut—get up, go to work or school, come home, watch television, go to bed. She thinks it would be exciting to travel.

In all of these cases, we see that the people seem to agree that "travel" has the basic meaning of "go from one place to another," but they don't all <u>feel</u> the same about traveling. When they hear the word "travel," they might really be thinking, "giving up friends," "freedom," "impress people," "too many problems," or "exciting." And "travel" might make other people think, "fun," "expensive," "tiring," "boring," or many other things.

Now you may be thinking, "So what does this have to do with critical thinking?" The answer is this: when a critical thinker is arguing with someone about something, he looks below the surface of the argument to see if he and the other person have the same <u>feelings</u> about the subject. If he finds that the feelings are different, then he discusses the reasons for the different feelings rather than the subject itself. In many cases it will then be seen that the arguments are based not on logic but on personal feelings.

CLASS EXERCISES

Problems 1-13: Complete each sentence with the first thought that hits you about it. Don't worry about whether or not other people may agree with what you write.

1. Police officers are _____ .
2. Television is _____ .
3. School is _____ .
4. Politicians are _____ .
5. Girls are _____ .
6. Boys are _____ .

7. Teachers are _____.
8. A good home is _____.
9. Smoking is _____.
10. Baseball is _____.
11. Doctors are _____.
12. Parades are _____.
13. Advertisements are _____.

Problems 14-22: Each problem gives a statement. Write one or two sentences to tell what <u>you</u> would mean if <u>you</u> made that statement.

14. "He's stubborn."
15. "She's stuck-up."
16. "He's conceited."
17. "She's bossy."
18. "He has a good sense of humor."
19. "That dress is expensive."
20. "I didn't have time to do my homework last night."
21. "That car is a lemon."
22. "That was a good meal."

3.4 A CHANGED DEFINITION MAY PRODUCE A CHANGED CONCLUSION

Suppose Fred is driving Clare home from school.

Clare: "Fred, you're driving too fast."
Fred: "No, I'm only doing 25."
Clare: "That's too fast. The speed limit here is 15."
Fred: "No, it's not too fast. It's safe to go 25 here."
Clare: "Anything over the speed limit is too fast."
Fred: "There's no harm in going 25 here. It's safe, so it isn't too fast."

Go back and read that conversation again. See if Clare and Fred are giving the same meaning to the words "too fast."

You should have noticed that Fred and Clare are giving different meanings to the words "too fast." Clare thinks that going over the speed limit is going too fast. Fred thinks that going a safe speed is not going too fast. He thinks that "too fast" does not depend on the speed limit.

Fred and Clare are not likely to reach agreement until they see that they are arguing about different things. For example, suppose Clare started out with, "Fred, you're going over the speed limit." Then Fred would have to agree.

You should notice a difference between this kind of argument and the kind of argument which may come from different <u>feelings</u> about a word. For example, we might agree that "travel" means "get from one place to another," but we might disagree about whether or not we personally like to travel. That is, we might agree on what the word <u>means</u> but disagree on how we <u>feel</u> about it.

However, we see that Fred and Clare do not agree on the <u>meaning</u> of "too fast." They both might feel that it is not good to go too fast, but they do not agree on just what "too fast" is.

Many times two people think they're both talking about the same thing just because they use the same word or phrase in their statements. But they may be talking about entirely different things. One example is the argument above between Fred and Clare.

We should be especially careful in arguing about legal matters. This is because we often need the <u>legal</u> definition, not the <u>dictionary</u> definition, of a word. Suppose part of a law reads, "A reckless driver shall have his driver's license suspended for not less than six months." This law isn't much good unless it also tells what "reckless driving" is, because different people have different ideas about what kind of driving is "reckless."

CLASS DISCUSSION PROBLEMS

Problems 1-2: Read the conversation and then answer the questions which follow it.

1. Miss Friday: "Jerry is a good student."

   Mr. Mensur: 'How can you say that? Jerry gets C's all the time."

   Miss Friday: "Yes, but he pays attention, and he studies the material. He uses the abilities he has."

   Mr. Mensur: "I think Brian is a much better student. He nearly always gets A's."

   Miss Friday: "But Brian only half-listens, and he doesn't have to study. Getting A's is easy for him. I don't think he's a good student at all."

   Mr. Mensur: "He must be a good student if he gets A's."

   a. What seems to be Miss Friday's idea of what "a good student" is?

   b. What seems to be Mr. Mensur's idea of what "a good student" is?

   c. Do Miss Friday's and Mr. Mensur's ideas agree on what "a good student" is?

   d. Make up an example of a student who would be called "a good student" both by Miss Friday and by Mr. Mensur.

2. Mr. Strawth: "Gene is a big discipline problem in my classroom. He's always asking a question or making a comment without raising his hand. He interrupts whenever the mood hits him."

   Mr. Waymore: "He does that in my classroom, too, but I don't think that makes him a big discipline problem. His questions and comments are always related to what the lesson is about. In fact, I think he does it just because he's interested in what's going on. I wish more students were like that."

   Mr. Strawth: "I can't believe you're serious. I can't imagine anyone's wanting more discipline problems."

   a. What seems to be Mr. Strawth's idea of a student who is "a discipline problem"?

   b. Does Mr. Waymore seem to agree with Mr. Strawth on this?

   c. In view of what Mr. Waymore said, how do you account for Mr. Strawth's last two statements?

3. Mrs. Vernan started out early for work. She decided to have some breakfast first, so she pulled her car into the parking lot of the restaurant across the street from the bank where she worked. When she finished breakfast, she thought there was no point in driving across the street to the bank, so she walked. She decided to go back to the restaurant for lunch, but when she got there her car was gone from the lot. She called the police to report her car stolen and was told that the police had towed it away. The officer said there was a "PARKING FOR CUSTOMERS ONLY" sign in the parking lot. He said Mrs. Vernan would have to pay a $35 fine to get her car back. Mrs. Vernan said she had seen the sign but shouldn't have to pay the fine, since she was a customer of the restaurant. The officer replied that she was not a customer of the restaurant at the time her car was towed away.

   a. Should Mrs. Vernan's car have been towed away? Why?

   b. Should Mrs. Vernan have to pay the $35 to get her car back? Why?

4. The speed limit signs in Littleburg were wearing out. The City Council decided to replace them with new signs showing the same speed limit. Councilwoman Bayert agreed and proposed that the new signs be made showing the speed limit in both miles and kilometers. The Council liked the idea. The new signs read

> SPEED
> LIMIT
> 25 miles
> 40 km

Mr. Dalland saw one of the new signs as he drove to the store. "It's about time they raised the speed limit," he thought. "They've posted the old limit as the minimum speed now. That's good." He drove at 35 miles an hour. He was stopped by a police car and was ticketed for speeding.

Should Mr. Dalland have been ticketed, or not? Why?

Problems 5-8: The city of Smallville was having trouble because there were many stray dogs running around. The dogs were becoming wild and were beginning to run in packs. So the city passed a law saying, "Any dog running loose in the city of Smallville shall be impounded." For each problem, assume that what happened took place in Smallville. Think about the law quoted above, and tell whether or not the dog should be impounded according to the law.

5. Ken's yard was completely fenced. He allowed his dog to run freely in the yard.

6. Mr. Maisden took his Chihuahua out for a walk each night. Mr. Maisden was tall, and the dog ran to keep up with him. Although the dog was on a leash, the leash was always loose because the dog always managed to keep up with Mr. Maisden.

7. Gary and his dog Duke had been through a 12-week dog obedience course. In this course, Gary learned how to teach Duke to obey certain commands. One such command was "heel." Given this command, Duke stayed on Gary's left side in a position so that Duke's eyes were in line with Gary's left foot. If Gary walked, Duke kept his position by walking. If Gary broke into a run, Duke kept his position by trotting or running. Whenever Gary took Duke out for a walk or run around the block, he didn't bother with a leash, since he always gave Duke the "heel" command as they left the house.

8. King was a beautiful six-months-old collie pup who had been abandoned when his owners moved to an apartment which didn't allow pets. King ran from door to door begging food and looking for his owners.

Problems 9-18: A city ordinance reads,
  It shall be unlawful for any person to keep, harbor, own, or raise any livestock, cattle, horse, duck, goose, chicken, goat, rabbit, snake, pig, or sheep in this city.

For each problem, assume the person is in that city when he does what the problem says. Tell whether or not the person is violating the ordinance. If you cannot decide, tell what you need to know in order to decide.

9. Mr. Traimer raises hogs in his back yard.
10. Mr. Arbor has a pet buffalo which he takes on walks around the block.
11. Jill has a Shetland pony which she rides in her big back yard.
12. Mrs. Brean keeps a pet rooster in her house and yard.
13. Mr. Rowler keeps a pet gander in his back yard.
14. The Carlands raise minks which they sell to fur processors.
15. Mr. Easen keeps bees in his back yard. He uses the honey they make.
16. The Nomars have a relative living with them. They are ashamed of him, for he is known as the black sheep of the family.
17. Mr. Plumber is a plumber. He owns a plumber's snake—a long flexible steel cable—which he uses to unplug clogged drains.
18. Chuck has a pet dog.

Problems 19-26: The Corber Public School District lists the following requirements for graduation from Corber High School (CHS):
  (1) The student shall earn at least 18 credits.
  (2) Each one-semester course successfully completed is worth ½ credit.
  (3) A course shall be considered to be "successfully completed" if and only if the student's semester grade for that course is D or better.
  (4) Credit for any one course shall not be earned more than once.
  (5) The student shall be required to register for at least eight one-semester courses offered by the CHS English Department.

(6) A two-semester course shall be considered as two one-semester courses for the purpose of these graduation requirements.

(7) A student will not be allowed to earn credit in the second semester of a two-semester course until he has completed the first semester of the course.

Assume that all the requirements for graduation from CHS are listed above, and assume that there have never been any guidelines issued which might help you to interpret these requirements. For each problem, assume that the student attended CHS, and do two things:

    a.   Answer the question asked and support your answer.

    b.   Tell whether or not you think your answer is consistent with the <u>intentions</u> of the people who made up the list of graduation requirements for CHS.

19. Kent has earned 20 credits, including 8 in English courses offered by the CHS English Department. Is he eligible to graduate?

21. Sheila wants to be an artist. She has taken and passed seven one-semester English courses at CHS. There are not enough hours in the school day to allow her to take all the classes she wants if she also has to take another English course. She reads the regulations carefully and decides she has found a way to get out of taking another English course. She registers for an English course. Then on the first day of class, she drops the course and signs up for advanced art instead. Assuming she ends up with 21 credits, is she eligible for graduation?

22. Alex has earned credit as follows: drafting, 4; physical education, 4; art, 4; shop, 4; machine shop, 4. Is Alex eligible to graduate?

23. Don's family moved to the Corber Public School District during the summer. Don completed 9th, 10th, and 11th grades at Webberville, 50 miles away. Don's records from Webberville show that he has completed 30 one-semester courses, including 6 one-semester English courses. All of his grades are C or better. What requirements must Don complete in order to graduate from CHS?

24. Nell goofed off in her chemistry class. She passed on a D. She knew that wouldn't look so good on her records when she applied for college, so she decided to take the course again. This time she got an A. According to the graduation requirements, which of the two grades will show on her final records, and how much credit toward graduation will she get for the chemistry course?

25. Ralph signed up for biology, a two-semester course. He put off studying for too long, and he ended up with an E for the first semester. He decided to stay in the course. He put himself on a strict study schedule and within six weeks was pretty well caught up in biology, including the material from the first semester. He ended up with a C+ for the second semester. How many credits will Ralph get toward the graduation requirements for these two semesters in biology?

26. Randy has earned credits as follows: English, 4; wood shop 4; gym, 6; choir, 4. Is Randy eligible to graduate?

27. By this time, you have probably decided that the CHS graduation requirements are not all they should be. Make a list of requirements for graduation which you think are reasonable. Include any guidelines which you think might be needed to make your intent clear to other people.

28. Speaking about some of the differences between Russia and the United States, John F. Kennedy said,

    The Soviets and ourselves give wholly different meanings to the same words—war, peace, democracy, and popular will. We have wholly different views of right and wrong, of what is an internal affair and what is agression, and above all, of where the world is and where it is going.

    Does this quotation have anything to do with what you're supposed to be learning in this section, or was it just thrown in to try to trick you? Explain.

3.5 DON'T JUMP TO A CONCLUSION— THE OBVIOUS ONE MAY BE WRONG

When faced with a problem, a critical thinker does not jump to a conclusion. He studies the problem, and then he asks four questions:

1. Is the information self-contradictory?
   (If so, forget about the problem.)
2. If not, is there enough information given so that <u>someone</u> in the world can solve it?
   (If not, try to figure out what other information is needed.)
3. If so, is there enough information given so that <u>I</u> can solve it?
   (If not, try to figure out where your own knowledge is weak.)
4. If so, what's the answer?

Sometimes the "obvious" answer to a problem may be the <u>wrong</u> answer.

Example:

Ms. Lowmer works in a dress factory. Her job is to operate a cutting machine. Each time she presses the button, the machine cuts off a piece of cloth two meters long. If she starts with a piece of cloth twenty meters long, how many times should she press the button in order to cut the cloth into two-meter lengths?

Answer that question before you read any further.

The usual answer to the question is "ten." But the correct answer to the question is "nine." We reason as follows: When she has pressed the button eight times, she has eight two-meter lengths of cloth cut off, or a total of sixteen meters of cloth cut off. This leaves her with a piece of cloth four meters long. So when she presses the button the ninth time, the machine cuts a two-meter length off the four-meter length of cloth, leaving her with only a two-meter length of cloth. So there is no reason for her to press the button a tenth time.

CLASS DISCUSSION PROBLEMS

Answer the question asked if you are able to do so. If you believe the problem does not give enough information for you to solve it, then answer "not enough information." If you believe the problem gives contradictory information, then answer "no solution."

1. A man buys a horse for $50, sells it for $60, buys it back for $70, and sells it again for $80. How much money (total) did the man gain or lose on these deals?

2. A grasshopper is trying to get a maple leaf from where he found it to a hole in the ground 30 feet away. The grasshopper hops 3 feet each time. However, the wind is gusty and very strong today, and every time the grasshopper hops 3 feet and lands, the wind picks him up and blows him back 2 feet. How many hops must the grasshopper hop to get the maple leaf into the hole?

3. Lily and Carmen both went looking for jobs. Lily was offered a salary of $10,000 a year with a raise of $1,000 for each year she stayed with the company. Carmen was offered a salary of $10,000 a year with a raise of $300 for each six months she stayed with the company. Assuming that both girls can stay with their companies for as long as they like, which girl was offered the better-paying job?

4. A man started out from his cabin and walked ten kilometers due south, then ten kilometers due east, and then ten kilometers due north. At that point he found himself back where he started, and he saw a bear which was native to the region sitting on top of his cabin. What color was the bear?

5. A man started out from his cabin and walked ten kilometers due south, then ten kilometers due east, and then ten kilometers due north. At that point he found himself back where he started, and he saw a bird which was native to the region sitting on top of his cabin. What kind of bird was it, if he did not start out from the same place as the man in problem 4?

6. You have two coins totalling 30¢, and one of them is not a quarter. What are the two coins?

7. If eight crows can steal eight buttons in eight minutes, how long will it take sixteen crows to steal sixteen buttons?

8. If eight crows can steal eight buttons in eight minutes, how many buttons can sixteen crows steal in sixteen minutes?

9. If eight crows can steal eight buttons in eight minutes, how many crows will it take to steal sixteen buttons in sixteen minutes?

10. Ms. Garjel wants to enter a race which requires a runner to complete two laps at an average speed of 24 km an hour in order to qualify for the race. During her first lap, Ms. Garjel got a cramp in her leg and ran only 12 km an hour. How fast does she have to run during her second lap in order to qualify for the race?

11. All boys have purple teeth. Aloysius is a boy, but he doesn't have purple teeth. How is this possible?

12. A father, a son, a grandfather, and a great-grandfather played a total of six games of chess. Each man won two games and lost two games, and there were no stalemates. How is this possible?

13. Fredericka, Georgia, and Hortense are a cook, a farmer, and an electrician. The cook has never been married. Hortense lives in the city so she can be near her work. The farmer's husband is also a farmer. Georgia, a widow, wants her 10-year-old daughter to learn her line of work. What is the occupation of each woman?

14. If a laying hen costs $15, how much will 4 dozen eggs cost at $1.10 a dozen?

15. Someone offered Beryl a job she wanted, but she was unsure of whether or not to accept it because of the pay. The pay was 1¢ for the first day, 2¢ for the second day, 4¢ for the third day, and so on, doubling each day for one month. Should she take the job?

3.6 EYEWITNESSES AND CIRCUMSTANTIAL EVIDENCE

An **eyewitness** to an event is a person who has seen the event happen. **Circumstantial evidence** for an event is evidence which tends to support the idea that the event happened.

Although great care should be taken to interpret circumstantial evidence correctly, such evidence is not subject to lies or to tricks of memory. On the other hand, the reports of eyewitnesses are subject both to lies and to tricks of memory.

There are two kinds of memory gaps. The first is the kind of gap we know is there—that is, we <u>know</u> we don't remember something. The second is the kind of gap we <u>don't</u> know is there—that is, we <u>think</u> we remember something which we don't really remember at all.

The second kind of gap is a big problem to us as critical thinkers, because it can fool us into believing that something is true when it is not true. Also, we cannot be sure that a truthful person is telling what really happened when he tells us about something he saw or heard or did. This person might really believe what he tells us, and yet his memory might be tricking him into believing that something happened which did not, in fact, happen.[1]

[1] Psychologists have said that the mind hates to have any missing pieces in an experience we are trying to recall and that the mind tends to fill in the blank spots with <u>something</u>. For example, suppose we're trying to remember something which had a first part, a middle part, and a last part, and suppose we really do remember the first part and the last part. Without our being aware of it, the mind will try to fill in the middle part. The "fill-in" may or may not be accurate. If it is not accurate, it can be either of two kinds of "fill-in": the first kind supplies a middle part which is not a true picture of what happened; the second kind simply ignores the middle part and leaves us believing that the last part happened immediately after the first part and that there was no middle part at all.

Because of such tricks of memory, we should be careful about believing what we hear from other people, and we should also be careful about being positive that we, ourselves, saw or heard something. Most of us are not usually paying full attention to what's going on around us. If something unusual happens, it takes a while to register on us that it <u>is</u> unusual, and by that time we've missed part of the action. If someone later asks us, "What happened, anyhow?!" we cannot be positive that our memories will be accurate.

And how about the way we remember people's faces? Have you ever seen someone and asked yourself, "Don't I know him from somewhere?" and then found out that you'd never seen him before? Or has someone you thought to be a stranger ever walked up to you and said, "I'll bet you don't remember me, do you?" Or has someone said to you, "You know what? There was someone who looks <u>just like you</u> at the store yesterday when I went shopping."?

I've had all of those experiences. Most people have times when they do not recognize someone they should recognize, and they have times when they "recognize" people they've never seen before. It isn't that they are dishonest—it's simply that their memories play tricks on them.

Summary:
1. Our memories play tricks on us.
2. Circumstantial evidence is not subject to tricks of memory.
3. Unless you were paying 100% attention all the time something was happening, don't be positive that you remember it exactly as it happened.
4. Unless you are listening to a trained observer, don't be positive that he is telling the truth even when you are convinced that he <u>thinks</u> he is telling the truth.
5. One person's face can look very much like someone else's face, so don't be too sure that you saw someone doing something unless you know that person quite well.

CLASS DISCUSSION PROBLEMS

1. Mr. Allander, known to be a truthful man and to have great respect for the law, was an eyewitness to a street robbery. Testifying on the witness stand, he said, "Yes, I know who did it. It was Christopher Yoram. I've known Chris ever since he was born. I was out walking my dog on Main Street, and I saw Chris and the man who was robbed standing next to the window of that little candy store near the corner of Elm—you know, that little store that has the red and white striped aluminum awning in front so that the sun doesn't get on the candies. Well, anyhow, it was a clear night, and there's a street light right there on the corner, so it was pretty easy to

see what was going on. Chris was wearing that new plaid shirt his sister bought him for his birthday the week before."

Would you tend to believe Mr. Allander's testimony, or not? Explain.

2. Ms. Ilmer slipped off her eyeglasses as she took the witness stand. "I was sitting at my desk by the window writing a letter," she testified, "when suddenly a man came running out of the front door of the Zaroch house next door. He was carrying a gun, and he paused for just a second or two and looked right and left. Then he ran and jumped into a car parked at the curb and took off." "How far were you from the front door of the Zaroch house?" asked the prosecuting attorney. Ms. Ilmer replied, "Oh, the houses are right next to each other. I'd say my window is about 10 meters from their front door." "Would you look around," the prosecuting attorney asked, "and see if you see that man in this court-room?" "Certainly," she said as she slipped her glasses on. "I never use them when I'm close up to something," she said to the prosecutor, "like when I'm sitting here just talking to you." Pointing at the defendant, she said, "Yes, that's the man. He's the one I saw running from the Zaroch house."

Would you tend to believe Ms. Ilmer's testimony? Explain.

3. Mr. Baring, who lived alone, was found slumped in a chair at the desk in his apartment. A bullet which entered his right temple had caused his death. His right arm hung limply at his side, and a gun bearing only his fingerprints was on the floor exactly where it would have been had it been dropped from his hand. Mr. Baring was right-handed, and there were no signs of a struggle. Mr. Baring had moved into the apartment about three months ago and was known by his neighbors as an honest, warm-hearted man. One of his neighbors said, "He was moody lately, though. Said he'd been married and that his wife had kept putting him down for his lack of education. Said he'd never gone beyond the third grade and that his wife had finally run off with a teacher. He said he'd sold their house and moved in here so that he wouldn't be reminded so much of her. Then about a week ago he said he still thought about her all the time and that moving here hadn't been the answer. He said he'd have to look for another answer." A typewritten note was on the desk:

I'm typing this note in order to save the reader of it the trouble of trying to decipher my handwriting, which has always been terrible.

Life has become meaningless to me since my wife left me. I have tried to forget her, but I cannot. I can see no point in continuing such an existence, so I have decided to end my life.

There is some money in my wall safe. Pease give some of it to the apartment manager to reimburse him for the expense of cleaning up the mess I am about to make.

74

The signature on the note was definitely Mr. Baring's. The bullet was recovered during the autopsy and was determined both to have followed a path consistent with the theory of suicide and to have been fired from the gun on the floor. Mr. Baring's registration for the gun was in his desk. When the wall safe was opened, it was found to contain $400.

Based on the information you have, which do you think more likely—murder or suicide? Explain.

4. Ms. Chopmore sat at her desk looking at the departmental final exam to be given to all students taking one of the department's courses. No one else was in the room this period, and she left the exam on top of the other papers on her desk while she went next door to check with Ms. Sartell about the wording of one of the questions. She was next door no more than a minute. As she came out of the room next door, she saw Keith, one of her students, coming out of her room. "Oh, hi, Ms. Chopmore! I was just looking for you," Keith said. "I wanted to ask you about something you said in class yesterday." Keith asked his question, and Ms. Chopmore answered it. "It was a good question," she thought. "I wish more students would ask questions like that." Returning to her desk, she found that the final exam was missing. She looked thoroughly for it, but it was nowhere in the room. Glancing at the windows, she saw they were closed and locked, just as she'd left them. She went to the classroom across the hall and told the teacher what had happened. The teacher, who was fond of Ms. Chopmore and was very reliable, said, "My class is taking a test this period, and I was just sitting here kind of staring into space when I saw you leave the room a few minutes ago. I kept my eyes fixed on your door. I guess I was waiting for you to come back. A couple of students went by in the hall, but only one student went into your room. I don't know him, but that's the student you talked to for a moment before you went back in. He was in the room for only about 20 seconds."

If you were Ms. Chopmore, would you think that Keith stole the final exam? Explain.

5. There was no doubt that Frank was driving his car when it struck and killed 4-year-old Betsy this morning. But the prosecutor was trying to determine whether Frank should be charged with manslaughter or whether this was just another unavoidable accident and Frank should be released. Frank's car had a muffler which did little, if anything, to lessen the noise of the engine; the car had orange and white flames painted along the sides; it had a raised rear end and extra-wide rear tires. Frank told the prosecutor that he had been going no more than the legal speed limit, 40 km an hour. Ms. Handur, who lived next door to Betsy and had been very fond of her, exploded when she heard this. "He's lying!" she told the prosecutor. "For years we've been seeing and hearing these cars driven by these kids roaring and racing up and down our street. We've called the police department and

complained about it, but the hot-rodders have always been gone by the time the police got here. We've asked for more stop signs and we've been turned down. I've always said that it would take a tragedy to wake up the officials in our city. Now I'm no judge of speed, but this boy, this Frank, I heard him come barreling down the street from a long way off, and I thought to myself, 'Here comes one that's really going fast! Too bad the police aren't here now!' He must've been going 70 if he was moving at all!''

How much weight would you put on Ms. Handur's opinion that Frank was speeding, and why?

6. Ms. Howerd called the police and reported that she had found her Aunt Heather dead. When the detectives arrived, they found Aunt Heather dead in her bed, with a tray containing two ordinary cookies and a cupful of lukewarm ordinary tea on the nightstand beside her bed. Her hand looked as though it was trying to clutch her heart, and her face still grimaced in pain. "What happened?" asked a detective. "I don't know," sobbed Ms. Howerd. "I suppose it was another heart attack. She'd just been released from the hospital three months ago after a nearly fatal attack. It scared her, and she said that starting right then she was going to do exactly what the doctor ordered. She said he told her what she could eat and drink and what she couldn't, and that he wanted her to start eating five small meals a day and have a bedtime snack instead of eating just three meals a day, and that she was to go walking regularly but was not to tire herself. He gave her a whole list of dos and don'ts. I thought she was doing so well! She seemed to be stronger each day! Just this morning she said that she was feeling so much better that she thought she'd go right on following the doctor's orders—said she'd finally got hold of a doctor who knew what he was doing, and she wanted to go right on feeling just as good." "How did you happen to go into her room?" the detective asked. "I heard her cry out," said Ms. Howerd, still sobbing. "I was in the kitchen fixing some tuna salad for tomorrow, and Aunt Heather came in and fixed her bedtime snack. She took it with her and then I heard her cry out two or three minutes later." "I don't believe you, Ms. Howerd," the detective said, "and I'm going to book you on suspicion of murder."

Why should the detective be suspicious of Ms. Howerd's story?

3.7 IMPLICATIONS AND INFERENCES

You **imply** (or make an **implication** about) something when your facial expression, your tone of voice, your mannerisms, or the words you use are meant to lead your listener to draw a logical conclusion about that "something." Any conclusions your listener draws from hearing and observing you are called **inferences.** The implication intended and the inference drawn may be two different things, for the listener may think you meant one thing when you really meant something else.

Example 1:

Drew: "My <u>brother</u> joined the <u>X-Group</u>?! I don't believe you!"
Drew's implications are: (1) I don't believe that my brother joined the X-Group; (2) I think you may be lying to me.

Notice that Drew has not implied that you, in fact, lied to him. His sentence, "I don't believe you!" is, logically, simply a statement that he needs more evidence before he can decide on the truth value of your statement. For example, if I were to tell you that the value of pi to 10 decimal places is 3.1415926536, you probably wouldn't know whether or not I lied to you. By telling me, "I don't believe you," you are saying simply that you need more evidence in order to decide whether I am right or wrong.

Example 2:

Drew: "My <u>brother</u> joined the <u>X-Group</u>?! You're lying!?"
Drew's implications here are: (1) I believe that my brother did not join the X-Group;[1] (2) I know my brother well enough to know that he would not join the X-Group; (3) you are a liar; (4) I have more faith in my knowledge of my brother than I have in your word.

In the next example, notice that the local neighborhood gossip has inferred something from Noreen's question which Noreen did not imply.

Example 3:

Gossip: "You know what I heard about that man Alta married? I heard he's a _____ ! I haven't seen him myself, but I've heard it from five different people now, so it must be true!"
Noreen: "Nice?"
Gossip: "Yes, <u>isn't</u> it, though! What a stupid thing to do!"
Noreen: "No, I meant, 'Is the man a nice person?'"

Because some people say things like "nice!" or "great!" when they really mean the opposite, and apparently because the gossip believes Alta should have married a different kind of man, the gossip has taken Noreen's question to be a comment of disapproval.

Summary:

1. A person who <u>gives</u> information is the only one who can <u>imply</u> something.
2. A person who <u>receives</u> information is the only one who can <u>infer</u> something.
3. The implications intended and the inferences drawn may be two different things.

---

[1] Notice the difference between this implication and implication (1) in Example 1 above.

77

CLASS DISCUSSION PROBLEMS

1. If a listener draws a conclusion from something said by someone, is this conclusion an implication, or is it an inference?

2. If someone frowns when he hears something, has he drawn an inference or made an implication?

Problems 3-6: Each quotation is followed by several lettered statements. Assume that the speaker meant what he said, and tell whether or not the quotation implies the lettered statement.

Example:

Problem: "My <u>brother</u> joined the <u>X-Group</u>? I don't believe you!"
   a.   You're lying to me.
   b.   I don't believe that my brother joined the X-Group.
   c.   I believe that my brother did not join the X-Group.

Answer: a.   not implied
   b.   implied
   c.   not implied

3. "Your <u>teacher</u> said that to you <u>in front of the whole class</u>?! Well, I'll just go to school tomorrow and get <u>him</u> straightened out on a few things!"
   a.   Your teacher should not have said that to you.
   b.   Your teacher should not have said that to you in front of the whole class.
   c.   Your teacher should find out that he acted improperly.
   d.   I have the right to go to school and try to make trouble for your teacher.
   e.   I will go to school in order to try to make trouble for your teacher.
   f.   I will talk to your teacher tomorrow about this matter.
   g.   I will talk to someone at your school tomorrow about this matter.
   h.   Your teacher should not treat his students that way.

4. "My <u>brother</u> joined the <u>X-Group</u>?! Wait 'til I get hold of him! <u>I'll</u> knock some sense into his head!"
   a.   I think you're lying to me about this.
   b.   I don't believe what you told me.
   c.   I believe you.
   d.   I do not approve of my brother's joining the X-Group.
   e.   I disapprove of my brother's joining the X-Group.
   f.   My brother showed a lack of good sense by joining the X-Group.
   g.   I'm going to try to convince my brother that his joining the X-Group was a mistake.
   h.   I would not join the X-Group myself.

5. "Genius is 98% perspiration and 2% inspiration."—Thomas A. Edison
   a.   What people call "genius" involves more work than brains.
   b.   It takes a lot of brains to be a genius.
   c.   It takes a lot of work to be a genius.

78

d. It doesn't take hardly any brains to be what is called a "genius"
   e. The average person could be a "genius" if he worked long enough and hard enough at it.
6. "Some laughed, others sneered and told me to forget it. They said that what I had in mind was the impossible dream, a task which only the most learned scholar would pursue. I was too ignorant to know that it couldn't be done—so I did it."— George Norman
   a. I did not believe people who told me that it was impossible to do what I wanted to do.
   b. I was not a learned scholar.
   c. I did something some people told me I was not capable of doing.
   d. If I had been less ignorant, I might have agreed with the people who told me that I was trying to do something impossible.
   e. Some people did not want me to do what I did.
   f. Some people tried to prevent me from reaching my goal.
   g. Some people told me that what I wanted to do was impossible for me to do.
   h. I was not discouraged when people laughed and sneered at me after hearing what I wanted to do.

3.8 CLASS DISCUSSION PROBLEMS AND QUESTIONS FOR CHAPTER REVIEW

1. Suppose someone has an equal number of red cards and white cards and mixes them thoroughly. If you draw one of these without looking,
   a. is it probable that you will draw a red card?
   b. is it probable that you will draw a white card?
   c. is it probable that you will draw neither a red card nor a white card?
   d. is it possible that you will draw a red card?
   e. is it possible that you will draw a white card?
   f. is it possible that you will draw neither a red card nor a white card?
2. Suppose someone has five red cards and four white cards and mixes them thoroughly. Answer the same questions as in problem 1 above.
3. a. What do you suppose is meant by the statement, "He's penny-wise and dollar-foolish"?
   b. Make up an example of someone who is penny-wise and dollar-foolish.
4. Do you agree with the old saying, "If a thing is worth doing, then it's worth doing well"? Explain.

Problems 5-7: For each problem, replace the blank by the letter of the most appropriate statement from among the following:

   a.   She's penny-wise and dollar-foolish.
   b.   Every cloud has a silver lining.
   c.   If a thing is worth doing, then it's worth doing well.

5. Mrs. Kanel's husband died last week from a heart attack. Her son smashed up the car the day of the funeral and is now seriously ill in the hospital. Her house caught fire yesterday and was completely destroyed, and there was no fire insurance on it. She has just received news that her best friend has an incurable disease and will die within three months. Another friend, trying to console her, says, "There's no sunshine in your life now, I know. the clouds have blotted out the sun. But just remember,_____."

6. Mr. and Mrs. Kobayashi returned home about 8 p.m. They had met after work, gone to a restaurant to eat, and then gone window-shopping. "I'm glad the kids are all at the basketball game tonight," Mr. Kobayashi said as they got out of the car. "I'm bushed. I can use a couple of hours of peace and quiet before they get home." "Me, too," agreed Mrs. Kobayashi. They stepped in the front door and gasped at the mess the kids had left. There were jackets, shirts, shoes, socks, and school books scattered around the living room. There was food left out on the counter tops and kitchen table. Apparently one of the kids had taken a bath and not cleaned the tub, another had taken a shower and hadn't wiped down the walls or the shower doors, and a third had used the wash basin and had managed to get water splattered all over the floor. "Well, I guess we'd better get started cleaning it up again," Mrs. Kobayashi said. "Not this time!" her husband replied. "Just leave everything exactly the way it is. The kids are old enough to clean up after themselves, so let them do it when they get home." About half an hour later, a car pulled into their driveway. "Good grief!" exclaimed Mrs. Kobayashi. "It's my boss and her husband! Let's get as much as we can of this mess straightened up before they get to the door!" "Forget it," said her husband. "You can't get it all done before they get to the door, so you might as well not do any of it, because_____."

7. "She saves all the buttons from her husband's worn-out shirts so that she doesn't have to spend money for new ones in case a button is lost from something else. But when she goes shopping, she goes for the latest fad, and then her things are out of style in six months or a year, so she just gives them away._____."

8. Do you believe that all old sayings are true? Explain.
9. List some of the feelings different people may have about the word "reading."
10. List some of the feelings different people may have about the word "parents."
11. Suppose someone asks you, "Do you think it's a good idea to have integration in our high schools?" What should you find out before you try to answer the question? Explain.

80

12. Take out a sheet of paper which is clean on at least one side, and do the things listed below in exactly the order they are listed. Do not say <u>anything</u> until everyone is through.

    (1) Write your name in the upper left corner of the paper.

    (2) Write today's date in the upper right corner of the paper.

    (3) Don't do anything else until you finish reading these instructions.

    (4) Nod your head if you understand so far.

    (5) Draw a triangle in about the center of the paper.

    (6) Multiply 14 by 10 and write the answer directly under the triangle.

    (7) Write the year Columbus discovered America in the lower right corner of the paper.

    (8) Put both hands on top of your head when you get this far.

    (9) Take your hands down again.

  (10) Add 45 to your answers to (7) above and write the total above the triangle.

  (11) Draw a square next to the triangle on the left side.

  (12) In the lower left corner of the paper, write the name of the first President of the United States.

  (13) Multiply the number you wrote above the triangle by the number you wrote below the triangle. Write the answer on the left side of the square.

  (14) Add your answer for (13) to your answer for (7). Write the total on the right side of the triangle.

  (15) Write the date of your birth between your answer to (12) and your answer to (7).

  (16) Clear your throat when you get this far.

  (17) Draw a triangle inside the square.

  (18) Write the name of this class under your name.

  (19) Now that you've read this far, go back and do only items (5) and (18). Then sit with your hands clasped.

13. Susannah: "ECONOCAR is the best car. It costs less to buy, it keeps its resale value better, and it gets better gas mileage."

Constance: "No, SUPER-8 is the best car. It's more comfortable, it's quieter, it seats more passengers, and it has better styling."

    (1) What seems to be Susannah's idea of what "a good car" is?

    (2) What seems to be Constance's idea of what "a good car" is?

    (3) Do Susannah and Constance seem to have the same idea of what "a good car" is?

    (4) At first glance, do Susannah and Constance appear to be talking about the same thing? Explain.

    (5) Are Susannah and Constance talking about the same thing? Explain.

14. a. What, if anything, did you learn from problem 12 above?

    b. On a separate slip of paper, write, "A critical thinker learns how to follow simple instructions." Take this paper home with you tonight and have the sentence tattooed on your forehead underneath the other three tattoos.

Problems 15-16: Tell whether or not the statement made is possible, and explain your answer.

15. Two men played five games of chess, and each man won three games. (A stalemate cannot be counted as a win.)

16. In my bedroom, there is a lamp which is 12 feet from my bed. Without using any extra aids (no wires, strings, or other devices of any kind), I can turn off the lamp and still be in bed before the room is dark. The lamp contains only one light bulb, and it is a very ordinary light bulb.

17. Describe one or two times when your memory played tricks on you. Do not include experiences of the kind where you forgot something and knew you forgot it.

18. "I think you'd better come over to my house," Mrs. Ebbdown told the police. "My husband's former wife just killed him." When the homicide detectives arrived, Mrs. Ebbdown told them, "I was taking a shower when I heard the phone ring. My husband answered it right away and the next second I heard him say quietly, 'I told you not to call me at home. She just got in the shower, and she always takes at least 20 minutes, so I can talk for a few minutes. Why'd you call?' He paused for a few seconds and then said, 'Absolutely not. No way am I going to see you tonight.' He paused again and was very angry when he spoke again. He said, 'If you come over here and make a scene in front of her, I'll never have anything to do with you again. I am _not_ going to see you tonight, and that's final.' Then he hung up the phone. Well, I was pretty upset, and I wanted to find out what was going on, so I hurried and finished my shower within a minute or two. I dried myself and was putting on my robe when I heard a car stop out in front. Just as I finished putting on my slippers, my husband's first wife came charging in and screaming, 'You rotten heel! You're not going to keep treating me this way!' Well, I came rushing out, of course. She was holding a gun, and she shouted at me, 'I'm going to kill him! And you get out of the way, or I'll kill you, too!' I begged her not to, but she was hysterical. She screamed, 'This is your last warning! Get out of here!' and she aimed the gun at me. I ran back into the bedroom, and I heard a shot. I was scared to come out and scared to stay there. But a second or two later I heard the screen door slam, so I came out. She was gone, and I called you right away." "You're going to have to think up a better story than that, Mrs. Ebbdown," one of the detectives said. "We're taking you down to the station. You'll be booked on suspicion of murder."

Why should the detective have been suspicious of Mrs. Ebbdown's story?

CHAPTER 4

COMMON ERRORS IN REASONING

4.1   CIRCULAR REASONING

4.2   ''PROOF'' BY SELECTED INSTANCES

4.3   AVOIDING THE QUESTION

4.4   SPECIAL PLEADING

4.5   FAKING A CONNECTION

4.6   CLASS DISCUSSION PROBLEMS AND QUESTIONS
       FOR CHAPTER REVIEW

4.1 CIRCULAR REASONING

You learned in chapter 2 what "premise" and "conclusion" mean. When someone comes to a conclusion which is logically the same as a premise, then he is using **circular reasoning**. Another way to say this is to say that **circular reasoning** tries to prove something by assuming ahead of time that it's already true.

Example 1:

　Avis: "Grass is green."

　Lisa: "Why do you think so?"

　Avis: "Because it <u>is</u> green."

In this case, Avis is using circular reasoning.

Example 2:

　Avis: "Grass is green."

　Lisa: "Why do you think so?"

　Avis: "Because it isn't red or blue or yellow, so it has to be green, because that's the only color left."

Avis is <u>not</u> using circular reasoning in this example. (She is wrong, of course, when she says, "That's the only color left," but her reasoning is not <u>circular</u>.)

　Circular reasoning is not always as easy to recognize as in Example 1 above.

Example 3:

　A good athlete must exercise regularly and be careful about what he eats. Therefore, attention to diet and a routine of exercise are necessary to a good athlete.

This, too, is circular reasoning. Although the second sentence <u>sounds</u> different from the first, the two sentences really say the same thing.

CLASS DISCUSSION PROBLEMS

Tell whether or not circular reasoning is being used.

1. You can't always judge a book by its cover. That's because a cover is not something by which you can judge a book.
2. You can't always judge a book by its cover. That's because the cover may be very different from what's inside the book.
3. People with big feet are often clumsy, but that's because people with big feet are often lacking in physical grace.
4. You should avoid all forms of contact with her, because you shouldn't have anything to do with her.
5. It doesn't make any difference to me whether you believe me or not, because I don't care one way or another whether or not you believe me.
6. Development of solid foundations of reasoning is essential to the proper education of a person. Therefore, if someone is to be educated properly, then he must at least acquire a thorough knowledge of the basics of reasoning.

4.2 "PROOF" BY SELECTED INSTANCES

In the title of this section, the word "proof" is enclosed in quotation marks to show that it is being used incorrectly.[1] When someone comes to a general conclusion about all things of a certain kind but he hasn't observed all things of this kind, then he is using **"proof" by selected instances.**

Example 1:

Chorng-Li, aged 7, has never heard his parents disagree. He thinks that married couples never disagree.

Example 2:

Marcus has bought many things advertised on TV and has never yet been satisfied with one of these products. He thinks that all TV advertisements lie about the products.

CLASS DISCUSSION PROBLEMS

Identify the kind of faulty reasoning used. If the reasoning is not faulty, then answer "not faulty." If you believe the reasoning is faulty but we have not discussed that kind of reasoning, then answer "none."

1. There must not be any good reason to study a foreign language, because I've never yet heard of a good reason for it.
2. I know I'm no good at foreign languages, because I've tried to learn two of them so far and have had a hard time with both of them.
3. You are probably unaware of what I am about to tell you, but that's because it is unlikely that what I am about to tell you is something you already know.
4. You said you'd let me go to the game tonight only if I did all my homework first, and I did all my homework first, so now you have to let me go to the game.
5. Socialists want to have all industries run by the government, and so does Senator Broading, so he must be a socialist.
6. There is hunger in the United States, China, Brazil, Egypt, and Spain, so there is hunger in every country of the world.
7. My mother can raise any kind of house plant. You should see all the plants she has—philodendron, ivy, African violets, begonias, geraniums—and every one of them is beautiful.
8. Mink coats are expensive, but that's because they cost so much.

---

[1] Recall that the word "proof" was also being used incorrectly in section 1.8.

4.3 AVOIDING THE QUESTION

Someone is **avoiding the question** if he understands the question but doesn't answer the question. We will count an "I don't know" answer as an answer, even though it may be a lie.

Example 1:

Mrs. Martz: "Is it serious, Dr. Kolum?"

Dr. Kolum: "It's too early to tell yet. We'll have to run some more tests."

Dr. Kolum is not avoiding the question. The answer given is a form of, "I don't know," which we said we would count as an answer.

Example 2:

Dawn: "Do you like my dress? I made it myself!"

Alix: "That's really an original design! I wish I could sew my own dresses. I've tried, but I always mess it up."

Alix has avoided the question. Saying that the dress is "really an original design" is not saying whether or not she likes the dress.

Example 3:

Fernando: "Dad, can I use the car tonight?"

Dad: "What do you think?"

Fernando: "Nope. You told me I couldn't use it again until next week."

Fernando's dad has avoided the question. Even though Fernando got his question answered, it was not answered by his dad. (To see this more clearly, suppose that the following happened. Suppose that Fernando had been goofing around a few days ago and that his dad punished him by saying that he couldn't use the car, but two days later his dad forgot the time limit he put on the punishment. So when Fernando asked his question in Example 3 above, his dad didn't really know whether or not the punishment was still in effect, and so his dad hedged by saying, "What do you think?")

The next example shows a form of avoiding the question which many people don't recognize. Read the example carefully and, before you read the explanation which follows it, see if you can figure out why it's an example of avoiding the question.

Example 4:

"Kids today don't learn as much in school as kids used to learn. Back in the old days, the teachers were strictly business. If a kid mouthed off, whomp! He got a ruler on the knuckles or got paddled, and, believe me, he paid attention after that. If a kid skipped school, the truant officer was at his house the next day. The kids learned the three R's without any nonsense thrown in, and when they graduated, they knew how to read, and they knew how to write, and they knew how to do arithmetic."

Have you figured out why this is an example of avoiding the question? If not, try reading it again before you read the next sentence. The first thing we have to do is recognize that there is a question, and we find in the first statement an implied question: "Do kids today learn as much in school as kids used to learn?" If you haven't seen yet why Example 4 avoids the question, substitute that question for the first statement, and then read the rest of the example again. You should see that the rest of the example does not answer the question. The speaker talks about how schools used to be, but he does not talk about how schools today are. He seems to be answering the question, "Did kids in school used to learn?" In other words, the implied question is one of <u>comparing</u> two things—(1) how much kids in school today learn and (2) how much kids in school in former times learned—but the speaker has not compared the two things at all.

CLASS DISCUSSION PROBLEMS

Identify the kind of faulty reasoning used. If the reasoning is not faulty, then answer "not faulty." If you believe the reasoning is faulty but we have not discussed that kind of reasoning, then answer "none."

1. Patrick: "Sis, why was I named Patrick?"
   Sis: "Why ask <u>me</u>? Ask Mom or Dad."
2. Patrick: "Mom, why was I named Patrick?"
   Mom: "Ask your father."
3. Patrick: "Dad, why was I named Patrick?"
   Dad: "Because that's the name you were given."
4. Patrick: "Grandpa, why is the sky blue?"
   Grandpa: "Because orange wouldn't look as good."
5. Patrick: "Grandma, why is the sky blue?"
   Grandma: "I don't know."
6. Patrick: "Auntie, why is the sky blue?"
   Auntie: "Because when the light comes down from the sun and bounces off everything else and gets thrown back up to the sky, blue is the only color that's left."
7. Patrick: "Uncle, why do you think that baseball is more exciting than football?"
   Uncle: "I like the excitement of watching games of skill, and baseball is strictly a game of skill. I get excited when I see the pitcher trying to get a strike past a batter and when I see a batter not letting the pitcher get away with it. And I get excited when a fielder makes a flying catch or when he intercepts a grounder and fires it right on target to the second baseman. I think that it's a very exciting game!"
8. Patrick: "Why do you think I should study French instead of German?"
   Counselor: "There are several reasons. French is an easy language to learn. Between 50% and 70% of all English words are derived from French words, so in a great many cases you can look at a French word and know what it means just because it looks so much like the English word which means the same thing. The structure of the French language is very much like the structure of the English language, too, so it isn't a lot of work to learn how to put a sentence together in French."
9. Patrick: "Laree, will you go out with me tonight?"
   Laree: "Get lost!"

4.4 SPECIAL PLEADING

Special pleading can take two forms. In one form, it says, "It's OK for me to act this way, but it isn't OK for you, even though the conditions are the same." In its second form, it says, "I can act in two opposite ways and call them both OK, even though the conditions are the same each time." In other words, a person is guilty of **special pleading** when he is not willing to apply his line of reasoning in the same way all the time.

Example 1:

Ivan's dad told him that speed limits are set in order to protect people. He said that driving over the speed limit is dangerous and that if he ever caught Ivan driving over the speed limit, he'd take away Ivan's driving privileges. But Ivan has seen his dad drive over the speed limit plenty of times when there was no emergency.

Ivan's dad is guilty of special pleading. He says he doesn't want Ivan driving over the speed limit because such driving is dangerous, but he still drives over the speed limit himself. Apparently he thinks it's wrong for Ivan to drive dangerously, but it's OK for himself (the dad) to drive dangerously.

Example 2:

Mahala: "How come you won't let me go downtown by myself? You let Isabel go downtown by herself when she was my age."
Mother: "That was ten years ago, and things have changed a lot in the last ten years. The streets aren't as safe now as they were then."

Mahala's mother is not guilty of special pleading. She apparently has a good reason for not allowing Mahala the same privilege allowed Isabel.

CLASS DISCUSSION PROBLEMS

Identify the kind of faulty reasoning used. If the reasoning is not faulty, then answer "not faulty." If you believe the reasoning is faulty but we have not discussed that kind of reasoning, then answer "none."

1. Mr. Southwary explained to his class that their parents were paying good money for their education, and he said that class time should be used fully. He said that because the class is kept from getting as much done as it should each time a student comes in late, he would insist that any tardy student apologize to the class and explain the reason for being late. Mr. Southwary was late for class today, and he neither apologized to the class nor explained why he was late.

2. "We've been on welfare for five years now, but we have no choice: I've been completely disabled by an uninsured motorist, and my wife has been ill for the past six years. So I think there should be welfare aid for people like us, but I don't think there should be welfare aid for people who are able to work and are just too lazy!"

3. Salvatore: "I don't think you ought to spread stories like that even if they're true. They don't do anyone any good, and a lot of people get hurt."
   Lawrence: "You told me about the same kind of deal last week, remember?"
   Salvatore: "Yes, but you asked me about it, and I told you because I thought you wanted to know."

4. In a recent survey of college students, 80% of the students said that the government has no right to interfere with their personal conduct as long as that conduct isn't harming anyone else; 52% said that one of the duties of elected representatives is to pass legislation which is for the individual's own good.

5. X Company gives discounts on its products to its employees but not to the general public.

6. "It's OK with me if that cashier short-changes people, as long as she doesn't do it to me!"

4.5 FAKING A CONNECTION

Suppose that LARGE store sells to the Carters, and SUPER store sells to the Carters. Does it follow that LARGE store is SUPER store?

Or suppose that as a first step toward a modern transportation system, Big City has installed movable sidewalks and, so far, the sidewalks move in only one direction. On a movable sidewalk, you can go from Elm to Main, and you can go from Oak to Main. Does it follow that you can go from Elm to Oak (or from Oak to Elm) on a movable sidewalk?

If you answered "yes" to either of the two questions above, then you are using faulty reasoning known as "faking a connection." You are **faking a connection** any time you assume that one thing is connected to another just because they have something in common.[1]

Example 1:

A dog is an animal. An elephant is an animal. So, a dog is an elephant.

This reasoning fakes a connection. It says that dogs are elephants just because they have something in common.

Example 2:

Dumbo is an elephant. An elephant is an animal. So, Dumbo is an animal.

This reasoning is <u>not</u> faulty. It does <u>not</u> fake a connection.

---

[1] This kind of reasoning is also called "distributing the undistributed middle term."

To see more clearly the difference between the reasoning in Example 1 and the reasoning in Example 2, we'll write both examples again, this time in a symbolized form:

Example 1: D is A. E is A. So D is E. (faking a connection)

Example 2: D is E. E is A. So D is A. (not faking a connection)

Do you see the difference in the two patterns?

Example 3:

All garages are buildings. You live in a building. So you live in a garage.

This reasoning is faking a connection.

Example 4:

All garages are buildings. You live in a garage. So you live in a building.

This reasoning is _not_ faking a connection.

Example 5:

All socialists favor government-run industries. Raymond favors government-run industries. So Raymond is a socialist.

This reasoning fakes a connection.

Example 6:

All socialists favor government-run industries. Raymond is a socialist. So Raymond favors government-run industries.

This reasoning does _not_ fake a connection.

Study the six examples above so that you learn to recognize the _pattern_ of reasoning which fakes a connection. This type of reasoning is often found in "transfer," a propaganda technique which is discussed in section 5.4.

CLASS DISCUSSION PROBLEMS

Tell whether or not the reasoning used is faking a connection.

1. Giraffes have long necks, and swans have long necks, so giraffes are swans.
2. Barns are red buildings. Some houses are red buildings. So, some houses are barns.
3. Barns are red buildings. Some red buildings are houses. So, some barns are houses.
4. Barns are red buildings. All red buildings are houses. So, barns are houses.
5. Old-fashioned people want to cut out the frills in education. Mr. Jaywin wants to cut out the frills in education. So, Mr. Jaywin is old-fashioned.
6. Police officers enforce the law. A sheriff enforces the law. So, a sheriff is a police officer.
7. All fire fighters are brave people. All fire fighters are dependable. So, all brave people are dependable.
8. These people are unreasonable in their demands. Radicals are unreasonable in their demands. Therefore, these people are radicals.
9. Mink coats are beautiful, and fur coats are beautiful, so mink coats are fur coats.

92

10. Good cars are always quiet-running cars, and the SUPER-8 is always a quiet-running car, so the SUPER-8 car must be a good car.

4.6 CLASS DISCUSSION PROBLEMS AND QUESTIONS FOR CHAPTER REVIEW

1. Suppose you ask someone a question and he knows the answer to it, but he answers, "I don't know." Is he avoiding the question, or not?
2. Suppose a scientist conducts the same experiment thousands of times and every time he gets exactly the same results. If he then concludes that these will be the results every time the exact same experiment is conducted, is he using "proof" by selected instances?

Problems 3-44: Decide whether or not the reasoning used is one of the following kinds of reasoning. If it is, then give the code for that kind of reasoning. If it is not, then answer "none."

Code	Kind of Reasoning
CR	circular reasoning
PSI	"proof" by selected instances
AQ	avoiding the question
SP	special pleading
FC	faking a connection
PC	proof by counterexample
PFFC	"proof" by failure to find a counterexample
SCP	substitution of a converse for its proposition
SIP	substitution of an inverse for its proposition

3. Joan: "Why should I want to do that?"
   Gwen: "Why shouldn't you?"
4. All the doctors I know who want socialized medicine are communists, so it must be true that all doctors who want socialized medicine are communists.
5. All doctors want socialized medicine, and Rae Tabner is a doctor, so it must be true that she wants socialized medicine.
6. All doctors want socialized medicine, and all communists want socialized medicine, so it must be true that all doctors are communists.
7. If a student doesn't fool around in class he'll learn more, because if he goes to class and pays attention then he's bound to get more out of the class.
8. Whaddaya mean, I'm never on time?! I was on time yesterday when we were supposed to meet at MacDonald's!
9. My daddy is smarter than your daddy, because my daddy's smarter than anybody!
10. She said I'd fail only if I didn't do any homework, so I did the homework and flunked anyhow. She lied to me.
11. She said I'd fail if I didn't do the homework, so I did the homework and flunked anyhow. She lied to me.

12. She said I'd pass only if I did my homework, so I did my homework and flunked anyhow. She lied to me.

13. June: "I don't think Rena should wear her skirts that short! That's positively indecent!"
    Anna: "But you wear yours that short!"
    June: "Yes, but I get tired of wearing slacks all the time."

14. "Dear Problem-Solver: I went to dinner at a friend's house last night, and there was a worm in my salad. I didn't know what to do, so I ate around the worm and talked to my friend as usual. What was the correct thing to do?"
    Answer from Problem-Solver: "Anyone who can keep talking to her friend as usual while eating around a worm doesn't need any advice from me."

15. I've never seen a teacher yet who wasn't a dictator at heart, so all teachers must be dictators at heart.

16. Girls are really fickle! I know, because I've known a lot of girls, and every one of them wanted one thing one minute and something else the next! There's just no pleasing them!

17. It's OK with me if people steal things, as long as they don't steal from me.

18. Mother: "When did Claude and Henry come in?"
    Father: "Henry came in first, and then I called Claude and he came in."

19. Not everyone who is smart is studious, because some people are smart and are not studious at all.

20. Good students are studious, and good students get A's. So studious students get A's.

21. Don't try to tell me that nobody ever gave you a break, because I remember last year when you got a job because your counselor recommended you to the owner.

22. My mother lied to me. She said I couldn't go if I didn't do the dishes first, so I did the dishes and she still wouldn't let me go.

23. You can't go to college if you don't get good grades, and you don't get good grades if you don't study. So you can't go to college if you don't study.

24. You can't go to college if you don't get good grades, and you can't go to college if you don't study. So you don't get good grades if you don't study.

25. Leo: "Why are you so stupid?!"
    Mac: "Well, nobody's perfect!"

26. Amalgamated Electric's (AE) products are really bad! We moved into a furnished apartment. It has an AE television, an AE dishwasher, an AE vacuum cleaner, an AE refrigerator, and an AE oven, and not one of them has worked properly ever since we moved in!

27. Free exchange of ideas among countries must be fostered if maximum scientific progress is to occur. Therefore, we will have the utmost in scientific advancement only if we promote the development of unrestrained trading of thoughts among countries.

28. Free exchange of ideas among countries must be fostered if maximum scientific progress is to occur. Therefore, if we promote the development of unrestrained trading of thoughts

among countries, we will have the utmost in scientific advancement.

29. Ms. Worner: "If there's anything that burns me up, it's people who cheat on their income taxes! If everyone would pay what he should, then my taxes would be lower. So in the long run, I have to pay more income tax just because other people cheat!"

    Ms. Jurway: "Yeah, me too! Say, remember that time your kid was playing baseball and knocked a ball through your picture window? You called the insurance company and told them some vandals had done it while you weren't home because you knew you wouldn't collect anything if they knew your own kid had done it. Did you ever collect from them?"

    Ms. Worner: "Yes, they sent me a check right away."

30. Student: "Mr. Ruband, what's the general formula for a circle?"

    Mr. Ruband: "I don't know."

31. Student: "How will you figure our grades in this course?"

    Teacher: "Oh, I'll be looking at different things—homework, tests, quizzes, effort, general attitude, class participation, attendance."

32. Student: "How will you figure our grades in this course?"

    Teacher: "Oh, I'll be looking at different things. Tests and quizzes combined will count as half the grade, and homework and class participation will each count as a quarter of your grade. If you're on the borderline between two grades, then I'll also consider your effort, general attitude, and attendance; otherwise, I won't consider those things in your grade."

33. I know that all fully-grown Great Danes are big, because I've never yet seen one that wasn't.

34. If a person is emotional about something, it's hard to get him to think critically about it. And it's hard to get most people to think critically about their religions if they attend church regularly. It follows that most people who attend church regularly are emotional about their religions.

35. Father: "Arturo, you should always wear your life jacket when the waves are this high. You're a good swimmer, but that wouldn't help you much without a life jacket in water like this if the boat overturned."

    Arturo: "You're not wearing your life jacket."

    Father: "No, I thought I'd get a little suntan first."

36. It's better to be safe than sorry. That's because it is not as good to regret something as it is to be secure.

37. This is a lousy area for getting decent TV reception. We've tried three different kinds of antennas and four different kinds of TV sets, and the reception has always been rotten.

38. That there is such a large number of high school graduates follows from the fact that so many people have graduated from high school.

39. My green-haired neighbor works twelve hours a day, so it isn't true that all green-haired people are lazy.

40. Beautiful women get a lot of attention, and so do enchanting women, so beautiful women are enchanting.

41. To try to talk sense to a man is stupid if he's angry. That's because when a man is not angry, then it isn't stupid to try to talk sense to him.

42. I'd be upset if my neighbors had guzzirs like mine, but I take good care of my guzzirs, and I don't think my neighbors should complain about my having them.

43. Melanie is in the first grade. She believes that all books have pictures in them because every book she's ever seen has had pictures in it.

44. Go back to the conversation in problem 1 of section 3.4. In view of the rest of the conversation, what kind of reasoning did Mr. Mensur use in his last comment?

CHAPTER 5

PROPAGANDA TECHNIQUES

5.1   INTRODUCTION

5.2   ''BANDWAGON''

5.3   REPETITION

5.4   ''TRANSFER''

5.5   ''TESTIMONIAL''

5.6   ''EXIGENCY''

5.7   ''FREE'' AND ''BARGAIN''

5.8   ''GLITTERING GENERALITY''

5.9   INNUENDO

5.10   ''NAME-CALLING''

5.11   MISCELLANEOUS TECHNIQUES

5.12   CLASS DISCUSSION PROBLEMS AND QUESTIONS
       FOR CHAPTER REVIEW

5.1 INTRODUCTION

Broadly speaking, **propaganda** is any rumor or idea or fact which is spread in order to convince someone of something. Propaganda may be truthful or not, and it is often one-sided.

Example 1:

Student: "What do you think of teaching high-school students?"
Teacher: "It's wonderful! The kids are settling down by then, and they have a marvelous sense of humor—not afraid to laugh at silly things, things which younger kids think they're too grown-up to laugh at. They have a big enough vocabulary by then so that I usually don't have to work too hard to get them to understand. They've outgrown things like throwing erasers or chalk or shooting paper wads. They're very easy to get along with."

Example 2:

Student: "What do you think of teaching high-school students?"
Teacher: "It's not for me. They can't be trusted. I never know whether a kid who smiles at me is apple-polishing or glad to see me. They'll make all kinds of oh-so-sincere statements and be lying all the time. I've even had kids tell their parents lies about me after I've spent months helping them on my own time with some extra project, and then the next day the parent came charging in to school ranting about my mistreatment of the kid and not even willing to listen to the truth."

We all run into propaganda almost every day, and this chapter is not going to tell you to try to avoid it. Instead, you will be taught some of the techniques[1] which are used by people who want to convince you of something. Then when someone uses that technique on you, you can recognize it and be more careful about letting yourself be convinced.

CLASS DISCUSSION PROBLEMS

1. Is propaganda ever truthful?
2. Is propaganda ever untruthful?
3. Is propaganda ever one-sided?
4. Does propaganda ever present more than one side of the story?
5. Can we avoid propaganda entirely?
6. Should we try to avoid propaganda? Explain.
7. Is propaganda harmful?
8. Is propaganda helpful?

---

[1]Each technique will be given a name. No name will be enclosed in quotation marks if the word "technique" follows it. But, to avoid confusion, some names will be enclosed in quotation marks if the word "technique" does not follow them. For example, you might be told any of the following: "Tell whether or not the bandwagon technique is used." "Tell whether or not 'bandwagon' is used." "Tell whether or not the repetition technique is used." "Tell whether or not repetition is used." In the second sentence of the preceding four sentences, "bandwagon" was enclosed in quotation marks so that you would know that the bandwagon <u>technique</u> was meant. In the last of the four sentences, "repetition" was not enclosed in quotation marks because the repetition <u>technique</u> turns out to <u>be</u> repetition.

5.2 "BANDWAGON"

One technique used in propaganda is called **"bandwagon."** The main idea of the bandwagon technique is "join the group."

Example 1:

   Ida: "Mom, Janie's invited me over to her house for a pajama party tonight. May I go?"

   Mom: "No, not yet. Wait until you're a year or so older. Then I won't mind."

   Ida: "But Mom, all the other girls in my class are allowed to go to pajama parties. Their moms say OK and let them go. Please, Mom?"

We see that Ida is using "bandwagon" on her mother.

"Bandwagon" may be used to make you think that if you don't go along with what's suggested, then you're old-fashioned, not up-to-date, or against progress—that is, you're not one of the group.

Example 2:

   Buford: "How about a kiss? Or two or three?"

   Carrie: "No, I'm saving my kisses until that Special Someone comes along."

   Buford: "Nobody's had that attitude for the past fifty years, so I know you're not serious. You just want to be coaxed a little, right?"

Buford is using the bandwagon technique on Carrie.

CLASS DISCUSSION PROBLEMS

For each problem, tell whether or not "bandwagon" is being used.

1. Telephone canvasser: "This is the X Home Improvement Co. calling. We know that your home is not a new one and that it probably needs some work done on it. We've been doing extensive home improvement work in your area recently, and several of your neighbors are having us in to do work on their homes now. We wondered if we might come to see you while we're in your neighborhood and give you a free estimate on the cost of doing any improvements you might have in mind?"

2. Teacher: "We're a little behind where we should be at this point, so over the Christmas vacation, I'd like to have you read pages 175-190 and do the exercises included in those pages."
   Student: "Hey, whaddaya tryin' to do to us? Nobody else gives us homework over Christmas vacation. Some of the other teachers were going to give us homework, but they changed their minds and told us to get a good rest and then we'd catch up when we got back. Can't we do that in this class, too, please?"

3. TV advertisement: "This offer expires at midnight tomorrow! Don't miss the opportunity of a lifetime! Order NOW!"

4. Advertisement: "Make your home the showpiece of your neighborhood! Call us today for a free estimate on remodeling your home!"

5.3 REPETITION

Another technique used in propaganda is repetition. The **repetition** technique repeats a word, phrase, sentence, or thought in the hope that you will remember it when you have finished reading or hearing the message being delivered. The hope is that if you hear something often enough, you'll believe it's true.

Example 1:

Advertisement:
"DO YOU WANT A CLEAN bathroom? USE MAGIC-KLEEN!
DO YOU WANT A CLEAN basement? USE MAGIC-KLEEN!
DO YOU WANT A CLEAN sidewalk? USE MAGIC-KLEEN!
DO YOU WANT A CLEAN kitchen? USE MAGIC-KLEEN!
DO YOU WANT A CLEAN garage? USE MAGIC-KLEEN!"

The message here is simple and direct. It is hoped that you will associate wanting something to be clean with the idea of using MAGIC-KLEEN.

The repetition technique may also be used to create an unfavorable impression.

Example 2:

Political candidate: "My opponent said he would work for better housing. But he voted against the Fair-Housing Bill. My opponent said he would work for better schools. But he voted against Bill No. 47, which granted federal aid to schools. My opponent said he would work for safer cities. But he voted against Bill No. 204 to provide federal aid to cities wishing to update their training of police officers."

Here, of course, the candidate is trying to create the impression that what the opponent said he would do and what he did do are opposite things. The candidate hopes that when you listen to the opponent's promises the next time, you will take for granted that none of his promises will be kept.

In both examples above, the words meant exactly what they said. But repetition can also be used when the speaker wants the audience to believe exactly the opposite of what he says.[1]

---

[1]For an outstanding example of the effective use of the repetition technique where the speaker repeats a thought but means exactly the opposite of what he says, read Mark Antony's speech which begins, "Friends, Romans, countrymen, lend me your ears," in Act III, Scene II of Sheakespeare's "Julius Caesar."

Example 3:

Roy: "Oh, sure, Mr. Lend is fair. Ira and I had the same answer on a test, and he marked Ira's right and mine wrong. But Mr. Lend is fair. He calls on some kids whose hands are up but not on others, so some get credit for class participation and some don't, even though all tried to participate. But, sure, Mr. Lend is fair."

CLASS DISCUSSION PROBLEMS

Tell whether the technique used is "bandwagon," repetition, a combination of both, or neither one.

1. "For a sparkling glow, for a sparkling smile, for sparkling teeth—use SPARKLE toothpaste!"
2. "You don't mean that! After all you've been through! You're not serious. You've worked too hard to quit now. You're just saying that because you're discouraged now, but you'll feel different about it after a good night's sleep. You'll change your mind, I know."
3. "Join the group of neighbors who've called us! Join the group of friends who've called us! Join the group of fellow-citizens who've called us! Join the group! Call us!"
4. "Make your home the showpiece of your neighborhood! Call us today for a free estimate on remodeling your home!"
5. Advertisement:

SUPERGAS
AMERICA'S NO. 1 GASOLINE!
Over 50,000 drivers a minute stop for SUPERGAS,
America's best-selling gasoline. Join the horde of other
Americans who have made SUPERGAS the gasoline
used by more people than any other brand.
Buy SUPERGAS today!

6. "This offer expires at midnight tomorrow! Don't miss the opportunity of a lifetime! Order NOW!"

5.4 "TRANSFER"

The **transfer** technique is being used in propaganda when the speaker (or advertisement or whatever) hopes to get your feelings about one thing transferred to another thing.

Example 1:

A TV advertisement for the nation-wide CHEAP restaurant chain shows a family of four sitting in "another restaurant." They sit at a dirty table and they wait for service. The waiter is indifferent about taking their orders. They wait for their food, and the orders are not brought at the same time. The kids are fidgeting through the whole thing. The prices are high. The scene then shifts to a CHEAP restaurant. The family walks in and sits at a clean table. The waiter comes immediately to take their order. He is courteous, smiling, and helpful. He brings the food almost immediately, and all the family are served at the same time. The kids are happy. The prices are reasonable.

The object of the ad is to get you to transfer your <u>negative</u> feelings about eating at a restaurant to a <u>competitor's</u> restaurant and, at the same time, get you to transfer your <u>positive</u> feelings about eating at a restaurant to a CHEAP restaurant.

Example 2:

A magazine ad for weight-lifting equipment shows a picture of a pretty woman in a bikini admiring some of the equipment.

Since women don't usually buy weight-lifting equipment, we see that a woman has little or no connection with the product being sold. But men like pretty women, and the advertiser hopes the man will transfer his feeling of interest and attention from the woman pictured to the weight-lifting equipment in the same picture.

CLASS DISCUSSION PROBLEMS

Problems 1-6: Tell which propaganda techniques are used in each problem. If a problem doesn't use any technique we've discussed so far in this chapter, then answer "none."

1. "The excitement of Paris! The elegance of the Taj Mahal! The mystery of the Orient! You'll know how devastating you can <u>really</u> be only if you're daring enough to try EXOTIC SCENT!"

2. "My opponent supports federal subsidies to farmers, federal aid to schools, a federally-funded program for guaranteed minimum income, and federal regulations for interstate commerce. These things, my friends, are exactly the things supported by the communists who have secretly wormed themselves into our government! Communist Russia stated years ago that communism would stamp out democracy! And how can we keep it from happening if we are unthinking enough to elect members of the Communist Party to our congress? We can't! So wake up, fellow Americans! Vote against my opponent! A vote for me is a vote against communism!"

3. An ad shows two pictures side by side. Across the top is the heading, "WHICH WOMAN DO <u>YOU</u> WANT TO BE?" The left picture shows a woman kneeling on newspapers spread in front of her oven. Her clothing and arms and face are smudged and dirty. Her hair is wrapped in a bandanna tied at the top, and wisps of stringy hair are hanging out. Sitting on the newspaper are a scouring pad, a box of detergent, a pail, a sponge, a can of BRAND X oven cleaner, and a can of BRAND Y oven cleaner. The woman looks exhausted. In the picture on the right, the kitchen is bright and sparkling. The woman is wearing jewelry and a party dress and her hair is gorgeous. She is sitting leisurely at the kitchen table talking

on the telephone while absently smiling at a can of CLEAN-GUARD oven cleaner she is holding. Underneath the pictures we read, "THE CHOICE IS YOURS. BUY CLEAN-GUARD TODAY!"

4. An ad shows a picture of a CLEAR-PIC television set. A pretty woman is standing beside it, smiling and resting her hand on its top. "The best in television quality—CLEAR-PIC!" appears near the bottom of the picture.
5. "Make your home the showpiece of the neighborhood! Call us today for a free estimate on remodeling your home!"
6. "This offer expires at midnight tomorrow! Don't miss the opportunity of a lifetime! Order NOW!"

7. Go back to the ad in problem 1 above.
   a. Opal is daring enough to try EXOTIC SCENT. Does the ad tell her that she'll know how devastating she can really be? Does the ad tell her that she won't know how devastating she can really be?
   b. Renaldo is not daring enough to try EXOTIC SCENT. Does the ad tell him that he will know how devastating he can really be? Does the ad tell him that he won't know how devastating he can really be?
   c. Hideki knows how devastating he can really be. Does the ad tell him that he's daring enough to try EXOTIC SCENT?
   d. Leota doesn't know how devastating she can really be. Does the ad tell her that she's not daring enough to try EXOTIC SCENT?
   e. Chloe used EXOTIC SCENT but still didn't find out how devastating she could really be. Did the ad lie to her?
   f. Dwight didn't use EXOTIC SCENT, but he found out how devastating he could really be, anyhow. Did the ad lie to him?

8. Go back to problem 2 above.
   a. Did the speaker <u>say</u> that his opponent was a communist?
   b. Did the speaker <u>imply</u> that his opponent was a communist?
   c. Did the speaker hope his listeners would infer that his opponent was somehow linked with communism? Explain.
   d. What kind of faulty reasoning did the speaker seem to hope his listeners would use?

5.5 "TESTIMONIAL"

The **testimonial** technique is being used when a famous person or a person in a position of prestige speaks in favor of an idea (or a product, or whatever). If only two choices are available—for example, if you must be either in favor of something or against it—then the **testimonial** technique is also being used when such a person speaks against the opposing idea.

Every use of "testimonial" also has the transfer technique built in, for the hope of the sponsor of the famous person is that you will transfer your admiration or respect for the famous person to the idea the famous person is supporting. We will call the technique "testimonial" if the famous person says something about the idea, and we will call the technique "transfer" if the famous person doesn't say anything about the idea.

Example 1:

Bonnie Beautiful, the internationally-known movie actress, is pictured with her hands on the arm of a handsome man. Across the picture are the words, "'No woman can resist a man who wears EXOTIC SCENT,' says Bonnie Beautiful."

This advertisement is using the testimonial technique.

Example 2:

The picture is the same as in Example 1 above. Across the picture are the words, "No woman can resist a man who wears EXOTIC SCENT."

This advertisement is using the transfer technique. The ad made no claim that Bonnie Beautiful had said anything about the product, so this is not an example of "testimonial."

As you can probably guess, the testimonial technique can be used whether or not the famous person has any expert knowledge about the idea (or product, or whatever). For example, a famous jockey might give a testimonial for an automobile and not know any more about automobiles than the average person.

CLASS DISCUSSION PROBLEMS

Problems 1-6: Tell which techniques are being used in each problem. If no technique is being used which we have discussed so far, then answer "none."

1. "This offer expires at midnight tomorrow! Don't miss the opportunity of a lifetime! Order NOW!"
2. The announcer says, "What do you think about SPRAY-ON rug shampoo, Arnie?" Arnaldo Astronaut, Spain's famous astronaut, says, "I think SPRAY-ON is the best rug shampoo I've ever used. I think everyone should try it."
3. Nina Nobody, who is not famous and not in a position of prestige, is shown pouring GOODSOAP in her washer. She says, "I think GOODSOAP is the best laundry soap I've ever used. I think everyone should try it."
4. "Make your home the showpiece of the neighborhood! Call today for a free estimate on remodeling your home!"
5. The caption over the picture says, "Dr. Hsu, chairman of the College of Engineering at Famous University is happy about our new design. We think you will be, too." The picture shows Dr. Hsu smiling with one hand on the product advertised.
6. The TV announcer says, "People all over America are pleased with the new SUPER-8 [pictures are flashed on the screen showing various people and groups of people smiling at the SUPER-8], from the biggest [picture is shown of

Benjamin Basketball, famous basketball player, towering above the SUPER-8] to the smallest [picture is shown of a small baby looking at the SUPER-8 and gurgling happily]. Isn't that right, Zeke?" Zeke Zekell, the famous Olympics runner, is shown standing by a SUPER-8, and he answers, "That's right. You're so right!"

7. Suppose that an ad shows Harry Handsome, the movie actor, and Nina Nobody both saying that SEE-FAR telescopes are marvelous. To whose statement would you give the more weight in deciding whether or not SEE-FAR is probably a good telescope? Explain.

8. Suppose that an ad shows Dr. Rodriguez, Professor of Astronomy at Famous University, and Nina Nobody both saying that SEE-FAR telescopes are marvelous. To whose statement would you give the more weight in deciding whether or not SEE-FAR is probably a good telescope? Explain.

9. Suppose that the same Dr. Rodriguez endorses the SUPER-8 car. How much weight would you give this testimonial? Explain.

5.6 "EXIGENCY"

The exigency[1] technique is being used whenever the speaker tries to make you think there is a good reason to take favorable action within a definite (usually short) time period.

Example 1:

"You'll never beat this low, low price! This offer may never be made to the public again! Call us right now at QX 8-4800!"

Notice that the ad tries to get you to take immediate action. It doesn't seem to give you much time to check out the claim made by the first statement in the ad, does it?

Example 2:

"We sold 20,000 of these last week and 25,000 the week before. We have only 15,000 left, so you'd better place your order now!"

As you can see from the two examples above, the hope in using "exigency" is that the listener will infer that he has no time to stop and think about whether or not he really wants the product. It is hoped that he'll order the product now rather than take the chance of not being able to get it if he waits a while before ordering it.

---

[1]The word "exigency" means "condition of being urgent," or "condition of needing immediate action." It is pronounced "ek suh juhn see" or "ig zij uhn see."

CLASS DISCUSSION PROBLEMS

Tell which techniques are being used in each problem. If no technique is being used which we have discussed so far, then answer "none."

1. "This offer expires at midnight tomorrow! Don't miss the opportunity of a lifetime! Order NOW!"

2. "Make your home the showpiece of the neighborhood! Call us today for a free estimate on remodeling your home!"

3. "Inflation is raising remodeling costs at a never-before-seen rate! A $500 remodeling job this month might cost you $600 two months from now and $1,000 a year from now! If you have remodeling to be done in your home, don't wait until later when you may have to pay twice as much. Call us TODAY for a free estimate on your remodeling job!"

4. "Let us send the FORCE SCREEN MACHINE to you for a free 10-day trial. Use it as much as you like for 10 full days, and if you're not absolutely delighted with it, just return it to us undamaged, postage prepaid, at the end of the 10 days and owe us nothing. Orders will be filled according to their postmarks, and we can't guarantee how long the FORCE SCREEN MACHINE will be available, so send us your order TODAY!"

5. "Our Weekend Special is a KELTAG washer and dryer combination for the amazing low price of only $_____! You'll never again see an offer like this one, so come in to any of our conveniently located stores either tomorrow or Sunday and take advantage of this week's fantastic Weekend Special!"

6. Big City's television shows are interrupted by a special bulletin: "Half an hour ago, a devastating tornado struck Midvale, just 20 miles from Big City. Scores of people were killed, and hundreds—maybe thousands—were injured. Many of the injured have suffered huge losses of blood, and it is estimated that the Red Cross emergency blood supply will be completely consumed within two hours. The Red Cross has issued an urgent request to the public for immediate donations of blood of all types."

5.7 "FREE" AND "BARGAIN"

The **free** technique tries to make you think you'll get something for nothing. **"Bargain"** assumes you'll pay something but tries to make you think that what you'll get is worth more than you paid for it. Both "free" and "bargain" may be tied in with "exigency."

Example 1:

"These are only a few of the hundreds of items shown in our new catalog. Send for your free copy of our new catalog today!"

This is an example of "free." If there is a postage-paid business reply card with the ad, it costs you nothing to send for the catalog. You should read such a card carefully, however, for there may be a little note on it which says that you must pay for shipping and handling costs. "Exigency" is not used here, for the ad does not try to make you think that there is a good reason to act within a definite time period.

Example 2:

   "FREE!   FREE!   FREE!   FREE!

   An electric toenail clipper is yours free if your order is $50 or more! Use the handy order blank enclosed!"

This is an example of "bargain." Although the word "free" appears in the ad, the ad does not offer an electric toenail clipper free if you don't buy $50 worth of other things. In other words, the ad lets you know that you are expected to pay something in order to get the clipper. It is hoped that offering you the free clipper will make you think you're getting more than your money's worth. "Exigency" is not used in this ad.

Example 3:

   "You'll never beat this low, low price! This offer may never be made to the public again! Call us right now at QX 8-4800!"

You may recognize this as Example 1 of the preceding section. Both "bargain" and "exigency" are used in this ad.

CLASS DISCUSSION PROBLEMS

Tell which techniques are being used in each problem. If no technique is being used which we have discussed so far, then answer "none."

1. "Make your home the showpiece of the neighborhood! Call us today for a free estimate on remodeling your home!"

2. "Let us send the FORCE SCREEN MACHINE to you for a free 10-day trial. Use it as much as you like for 10 full days, and if you're not absolutely delighted with it, just return it to us undamaged, postage prepaid, at the end of the 10 days and owe us nothing. Orders will be filled according to their postmarks, and we can't guarantee how long the FORCE SCREEN MACHINE will be available, so send us <u>your</u> order TODAY!"

3. "Our Weekend Special is a KELTAG washer and dryer combination for the amazing low price of only $_____! You'll never again see an offer like this one, so come in to any of our conveniently located stores either tomorrow or Sunday and take advantage of this week's fantastic Weekend Special!"

4. "Call us now and ask for a copy of our free brochure explaining these things in detail."

5. "The helping Hand Society of Big City issued a public appeal today for volunteer drivers. 'We need anyone who has a car and two or three hours a week to spare,' said Ms. Tarkle, founder of the Helping Hand Society. 'We know of so many people who need medical treatment but have no transportation enabling them to get it. The volunteers would not be paid any money, but the gratitude of the people they help and the knowledge that they have helped someone else is more than enough.'"

6. "Make $50, $100, $200 a week in your spare time! For only $5, we'll send you the booklet, 'HOW TO MAKE MONEY IN YOUR SPARE TIME.' Send for this booklet today!"

7. "Look, we both agree that it was a mistake to hire your wife's brother. He doesn't do his work, he's losing customers for us because he's so rude, and he makes all the other employees nervous and irritable. We've both talked to him about his attitude, but it hasn't done any good. I know your wife won't like it, but we're just going to have to discharge him. It's better to discharge him and have your wife upset for a while than to keep him and let him ruin the business."

8. "Look, we both agree that it was a mistake to hire your wife's brother. He doesn't do his work, he's losing customers for us because he's so rude, and he makes all the other employees nervous and irritable. We've both talked to him about his attitude, but it hasn't done any good. So here's what we'll do. We'll call in each employee, including your brother-in-law, and tell him or her that we're thinking of reorganizing the work load for a more efficient operation. We'll ask for a detailed list from each employee of the duties he or she now has. You'll mention this to your wife when we start it. Two weeks later, we'll call in your brother-in-law again and tell him his job has been eliminated by the reorganization. Presto! We're happy, the other employees are happy, our customers are happy. Even your wife and her brother aren't mad at us, because they're convinced it was strictly because of business needs and was nothing personal."

5.8 "GLITTERING GENERALITY"

Some words or phrases glitter, or sparkle, or otherwise seem to draw your attention. When a speaker uses words or phrases which are attractive but he doesn't mention specific details, then he is using the **glittering generality** technique.

Example 1:

"Here's the breakfast cereal the world has waited for! It tastes better, looks better, and smells better! It's more nourishing and less expensive! Buy MIRACLE BREAKFAST today!"

This is an example of the use of the glittering generality technique. We'll take another look at this ad, but this time we'll look at it a little at a time: "Here's the breakfast cereal the world has waited for! [1] It tastes better [2], looks better [3], and smells better [4]! It's more nourishing [5] and less expensive [6]! Buy MIRACLE BREAKFAST today! [7]"

[1]: I thought the world had been going on as usual. I didn't know it was waiting for a new breakfast cereal. Do they mean that some people haven't been eating breakfast just because there was no good cereal available, and now these people will start eating breakfast?

[2]-[6]: than what?

[7]: The <u>name</u> of the cereal is certainly attractive, but, to misquote Shakespeare, "What's in a name? A bad apple by any other name is just as rotten."

The next two examples also use the glittering generality technique. Just to save repeating the ads later, the bracketed numerals are included in the examples but should be ignored while you're reading the ads.

Example 2:

"Four out of five medical doctors surveyed [1] said that they advise patients [2] to use MEDITABLET for temporary [3] relief [4] from minor aches and pains [5]."

[1]: How many doctors were surveyed? Five? A hundred? Or maybe they surveyed 1,000, of which 4 said "yes," and 996 said "no." If so, they could take one of the 996 "no" doctors for the fifth doctor and still claim that four out of five doctors surveyed said "yes."

[2]: <u>Which</u> patients? No doctor is going to say to every one of his patients, "You should use MEDITABLET . . .." So the patients who were advised to use MEDITABLET must have had some special medical condition at the time, and this condition may have no relation to my condition.

[3]: How long is <u>that</u>? Two seconds? All day? Until I can get to the doctor's office next week?

[4]: That could mean anything from getting rid of it entirely to lessening it by just the tiniest fraction.

[5]: What does "minor" mean here? Does it mean "relatively unimportant"? If so, I'm no doctor, so how do I know which aches and pains are relatively unimportant and which ones could indicate something really serious?

Example 3:

"This candidate has the background needed to be a good mayor [1]. He has workable, common-sense ideas [2] about better housing [3] and lower taxes [4]."

[1]: What background do they think is needed for this? What do they consider to be "a good mayor"?

[2]: That's nice. But what <u>are</u> these ideas? And is he <u>in favor of</u>, or is he <u>against</u>, the items listed?

[3]: Better than what? Better for whom?

[4]: Lower than what? Taxes on what?

109

2. "A leading laboratory [1] reports [2] that there was a statistically significant [3] difference between the health of dogs which ate only DOGBURGER dog food and dogs which ate only other leading brands [4] of dog food, with the DOGBURGER-fed dogs being the healthier." [5]
3. "Finally, the opportunity [1] of a lifetime [2]! The most talked-about [3] book in America today now at the unbelievable [4] price of only $_____!"

Problems 4-5: Each problem here is an example of "glittering generality," but this time no bracketed numerals appear. See how many things you can find to question.

4. "John X is the ideal man to be the mayor of Big City! He is a respected businessman, he has a legal background, and he has administrative abilities. Vote for John X!"
5. "Come to us for a real bargain price! If we can't sell it at the lowest possible price, then we won't sell it at all!"

5.9 INNUENDO

The **innuendo**[1] technique is being used whenever the speaker uses words in such a way that he hints indirectly (but doesn't come right out in the open about it) that the person he is talking about has something to hide.

Example 1:

"You all know that I'm a candidate for mayor in next Tuesday's election. I have asked our mayor to debate the campaign issues with me on public television, but she has refused. Now I ask you, why should she be afraid to debate the issues with me on public television? Is she afraid she'll be asked to explain her unkept promises? Is she afraid she'll be asked to explain exactly where she stands on the question of improved housing? Is she afraid she'll be asked why she supported a city income tax?"

This is an example of the innuendo technique. All four questions asked are examples of innuendo. Notice that the speaker never said that the mayor is afraid, but he certainly wanted us to think that (1) the mayor is afraid to debate with him on public television, and (2) the reason she is afraid is that she hasn't been a good mayor and doesn't want this brought out in the open. As you can see, innuendo can be very harmful to the person who is the object of it.

In the example above, a critical thinker would not jump to the conclusion that the mayor is afraid to debate the candidate on public television. Instead, he would ask, "Why might the mayor decide not to debate this candidate on public television?" Among the possible answers are these: (1) Maybe the mayor feels that the time she would have to spend preparing for such a debate could better be spent taking care of her mayoral duties. (2) Maybe there was only one time available on TV, and she was scheduled

---

[1] The word "innuendo" (pronounced "in yuh wen doe") means "veiled hint" or "insinuation" or "roundabout indirect reference."

to be in Washington, D.C. at that time to speak to a congressional subcommittee about the importance of federal aid to cities such as hers. (3) Maybe she is the kind of person who thinks slowly, and she has found that this slowness is often misinterpreted as a desire to evade the questions asked. (4) Maybe she hasn't been a good mayor and is afraid that this will be brought out in a public television debate.

Example 2:

"How are our kids supposed to learn how to read in elementary schools today when they spend all their time going to puppet shows and gym and music and art classes?!''

This question, too, is an example of innuendo. The speaker has not <u>said</u> that elementary school kids spend all their school time ''going to puppet shows, . . .,'' but the tone of his question makes it clear that he'd like us to think that's what they do with all of their school time. (Remember that the word ''when'' tells you that the sentence is an ''if-then'' sentence.) Apparently, the speaker is trying to convince us that elementary schools today are not teaching kids how to read, and the reason they're not is that they're wasting the school day on nonessential things. He has not <u>said</u> this, but he has used innuendo to get us to think it.

CLASS DISCUSSION PROBLEMS

Tell which problems are examples of innuendo and which ones are not.

1. "He claims he's innocent. Then why is he afraid to tell us where he was on the night in question?"

2. "Why does our City Council meet in closed sessions?! Maybe they're planning to give an OK on that new zoning law secretly so that we won't know about it. Maybe they don't want the public to know what they're planning to do in our city. Maybe they know the public would be outraged if everything were out in the open."

3. "Why does our City Council meet in closed sessions? Maybe they're hearing charges against a city employee which would embarrass him if the charges were discussed in public, and they don't want to embarrass the employee. Maybe they're discussing ways of conducting public meetings more efficiently. Maybe they're trying to find a way to balance their work load more evenly among all the council members."

4. "The BURPO POP Company announces its new diet pop—BURPO DIET POP. BURPO DIET POP tastes just like BURPO POP—good, <u>good</u>, GOOD! We notice that our competitors don't call <u>their</u> diet pops by the names they use for their regular pops. We wonder why not. After all, we're not ashamed to call <u>our</u> diet pop by <u>our</u> regular pop name—BURPO DIET POP! Get some today!"

5. "Now how come Johnwell got the job when he doesn't know the business as well as Ebisu? It wouldn't have anything to do with the fact that Johnwell has an American-sounding name, while Ebisu has a Japanese-sounding name, would it? It

wouldn't be because the company's biggest customer called up and just happened to mention that he would find it very difficult to do business with anyone with a Japanese name, would it? And, of course, the fact that the chairman of the board just happens to dislike <u>all</u> Orientals wouldn't make any difference, would it?''

5.10 ''NAME-CALLING''

The **name-calling** technique is being used whenever the speaker tries to get you to agree with him by referring to certain people as part of an undesirable large mass or group rather than as individuals. ''**Name-calling**'' is designed to stop your thinking processes and get you to react <u>emotionally</u> instead of <u>logically</u>.

Let's start out by looking at the same question from two opposing viewpoints. In each case, the speaker is using the name-calling technique.

Example 1:

''You can see what these self-righteous book banners are trying to do to us! They're trying to set themselves up as dictators over us, telling us what kinds of books we can buy and what kinds we can't! No self-respecting American is going to sit by and let these self-appointed censors come along and tell him that the Bill of Rights in our U.S. Constitution doesn't guarantee us freedom of the press!''

You can see that if we leave out all the emotionalism, the speaker has merely said, ''Some people want to keep certain kinds of books from being sold.'' He has given us no details about the kinds of books, and he has given us no <u>logical</u> reason for disagreeing with these people.

Now let's look at the other side of the question.

Example 2:

''Are we going to sit idly by and let such filthy trash be sold right here in the heart of the United States of America?! The people who want to buy these books, the ones with the degenerate, perverted minds, actually expect the rest of us—the good, honest, hard-working Americans—to help them corrupt our American ideals by allowing such garbage to be sold!''

Leaving out all of the emotionalism, the speaker has merely said, ''I think that certain kinds of books should not be sold.'' Like the first speaker, he has given us no details about the kinds of books, and he has given us no <u>logical</u> reason for thinking as he does.[1]

Let's take a look at some of the words and phrases designed to cause an emotional reaction rather than a logical reaction. We'll list them as ''good'' or ''bad,'' according to whether or not most Americans would react favorably to the thing described.

---

[1]You may have noticed from Examples 1 and 2 that the name-calling technique may also have innuendo built in.

112

Good:	Bad:
self-respecting American	self-righteous
Bill of Rights	book banners
U.S. Constitution	dictators
freedom of the press	self-appointed censors
heart of the United States of America	filthy trash
good, honest, hard-working Americans	degenerate, perverted minds
American ideals	corrupt
	garbage

Each time you hear someone use such words and phrases, you should stop and ask yourself whether the words or phrases are being used <u>logically</u> or whether they are being used <u>emotionally</u>.

Our language has many slang terms—most of which are used only as put-downs—for people of other races, religions, colors, or national origins. Such words include, for example, "whitey," "hunky," "honky," "bohunk," "nigger," "coon," "Chink," "limey," "mick," "wop," "Polack," "Russky," "Red," "Jap," "Buddha-lover," "heathen," "slant-eyes," "Yid," "kike," "spick," "pope-lover," "Kraut," and "greaser." Whenever you hear someone use a word like one of these, stop and think about what he's saying, for chances are excellent that he's trying to convince you of something on an emotional level rather than on a logical level. If he were trying to convince you by logic, chances are good that he'd use "German" instead of "Kraut," "Negro" instead of "nigger," "Caucasian" instead of "whitey," and so on.

CLASS DISCUSSION PROBLEMS

Tell which techniques are being used in each problem. If the technique used is "name-calling," then summarize the speaker's main idea in one relatively short sentence. If no technique discussed so far is being used, then answer "none."

1. "If you elect me, I'll work for reform of the laws that give away our tax money to the shiftless freeloaders and call it 'welfare aid'! Every good American has always believed in giving an honest day's work for an honest day's pay! No one has to come along with any free handouts for your solid American citizen! No sir, all of us nephews and nieces of Uncle Sam are willing to work for what we get, and we don't need laws that take our hard-earned money away from us in taxes and then turn around and give it away to some lazy good-for-nothing sponge who isn't willing to work!"

2. "Americans have to start standing up for the American way of life! We're letting a bunch of aliens take over our country! Our beautiful country is being flooded with products made by Krauts, wops, and Japs, and all of these foreigners are selling the products for less here than they do in their own countries! There's only one reason they'd do that, and that's because they're trying to take over America!"

3. "Whitey says we should wait! Whitey says we shouldn't push too hard! Well, I say we've waited long enough! I say that uppity whitey still thinks we're his slaves and that we should bow and scrape and answer 'Yassuh!' whenever he snaps his fingers! Even our college graduates have a hard time getting jobs because whitey won't give a black man a chance! It's time we stopped letting these honkies treat us like fifth-class citizens! It's time we stopped settling for fifth-rate jobs!"

4. "Are we going to let these niggers take jobs away from white men?! Nobody went to our bosses and told them they had to hire us, but that's because they knew that white men are willing to work for their pay! Everyone knows that niggers are lazy and shiftless and that a coon doesn't have the ability a white man has! It's downright stupid to hire a nigger when a white man's willing to take the job!"

5.11 MISCELLANEOUS TECHNIQUES

There are many other techniques which are used in propaganda. Some speakers are guilty of errors in reasoning such as those already discussed in chapters 1-4. Some speakers draw unsupported conclusions. You were exposed to some of the ideas involving unsupported conclusions in chapters 1-4, and we'll go into this more carefully in chapter 7. Some speakers mix facts and opinions very skillfully, and they don't tell you that the opinions are opinions. In chapter 7, we'll also take a closer look at the use of emotional words and phrases in everyday life. You saw a lot of emotional words and phrases used in connection with the name-calling technique, but emotional words and phrases can also be used to try to influence you about something when there is no name-calling involved.

When the **card-stacking** technique is used, only one side of an issue is presented.

Example 1:

Every high school student in the United States should take at least two years of a foreign language. First, such study is good for disciplining the mind. Second, the comparison of a foreign language with English gives the student a better knowledge of the structure of English. Third, the student gets a better understanding of another country by studying its language. Fourth, there are more jobs open to someone who speaks two languages than to someone who doesn't.

There are more reasons which could be listed, of course, but you get the idea—the other side of the question is never even mentioned. A critical thinker will automatically ask, "And what are some good reasons to oppose this idea?" He does not take for granted that one side has no good reasons to support it just because the other side has many good reasons to support it. You'll be asked to think of good reasons for two sides of various issues in chapter 8.

Another propaganda technique used is **oversimplifying.** Here, the speaker leaves out some of the problems you might run into if you go along with his idea.

114

Example 2:

Automobiles are causing too much air pollution. To correct this, all we have to do is pass a federal law telling the car manufacturers that within five years, all new cars manufactured must burn fuel with 100% efficiency. Then there'll be no exhaust from the new cars. At the same time, we'll pass another another federal law banning all cars more than ten years old. Then in fifteen years, there will be no air pollution at all from cars.

The **snob** technique is being used when the speaker tries to make you think that going along with his idea will somehow make you more noteworthy than the average person.

Example 3:

"Make your home the showpiece of the neighborhood! Call us today for a free estimate on remodeling your home!"

As you learned in problem 1 of section 5.7, this ad is an example of "free," as far as the remodeling estimate is concerned. But the first sentence of the ad is strictly "snob." "Testimonial" (and, sometimes, "transfer") also has a certain amount of "snob" built in, for some people tend to think, for example, that if they use the same product that Harry Handsome uses, then they're somewhat like Harry Handsome.

Although the snob technique appeals to many people, there are also many people who, if not turned off by it, are at least unmoved by it. But such people are sometimes influenced by the **just plain folks** technique, which is the opposite of "snob."

Example 4:

"Hi, everybody! I'm Nina Nobody. I'm just an average woman who works in an office. Before I started using HARD NAILS, it seemed like I was breaking fingernails twice a week. You know how it is—typing, filing, dialing a phone, cleaning the house when I got home from work. But then I started using HARD NAILS, and just look at my beautiful nails now!"

Still another propaganda technique is "flag-waving." The **flag-waving** technique tries to make you think that you're patriotic if you go along with what's suggested and you're unpatriotic if you don't. "Flag-waving" is usually tied in with at least one other propaganda technique. As examples, "flag-waving" is used with "transfer" in problem 2 of section 5.4, and it is used with "name-calling" in Examples 1 and 2 and in problems 1 and 2 of section 5.10.

CLASS DISCUSSION PROBLEMS

1. Go back to Example 1 in section 5.1. What propaganda technique is being used here?
2. Go back to Example 2 in section 5.1. What propaganda technique is being used here?

Problems 3-7: For each problem, tell what technique is being used. If no technique discussed is being used, then answer "none."

3. Letter received in the mail: "Your daughter has been recommended to us for the outstanding honor of having her name

included in our new edition of *Who's Who Among the World's Teenagers*. Because we never reprint an edition, it may be that you will be unable to buy a copy once it is off the press. Yet, we know you'd like to have a copy to keep as a treasured memento during the years to come. For this reason, we are offering to reserve a copy for you now. The cost of this beautifully-bound volume is only $50, and it will be shipped to you in about three months. . . ."

4. Salesperson: "My boss told me not even to bother with this street. He said the people here wouldn't be able to afford a really good product like this. But I told him I was going to try it anyhow. I said, 'Look, Mr. Barnwill, people who don't have money to waste are the very ones who should buy this. Otherwise, they'll go out and keep buying cheap brands that wear out in six months, and they'll end up spending two or three times as much. They know the real value of money, and they'll know they're money ahead to buy our product.'"

5. Letter to the editor of a newspaper: "I don't see what all the fuss is about over the increase in crime. It's been on the increase ever since the public whipping post was abandoned. If we restored the public whipping post as a punishment for crime, believe me, the crime rate would go down in a hurry, because no criminal would want to be whipped in public!"

6. "My name is Lonnie Yarwell. I'm a truck driver. I think I should have a cast-iron stomach after eating at so many roadside diners, but my stomach doesn't agree with that and it tries to give me a rough time once in a while just to prove it. But I just laugh and say, 'Take that, stomach!' and I drink a glass of URPO-SELTZER. It works for my stomach, and if it works for mine, it'll work for yours."

7. A political candidate is photographed at Polish wedding receptions, class reunions, veteran's dinners, family picnics, and at ethnic festivals. He is also photographed while shopping in a local shopping center and while mowing his lawn.

5.12 CLASS DISCUSSION PROBLEMS AND QUESTIONS FOR CHAPTER REVIEW

1. Suppose there are only two products on the market—BRAND X and BRAND Y—which will do a certain job. And suppose a BRAND X advertisement shows a famous engineer speaking at an engineering convention about the dangers of using BRAND Y because of faulty engineering. Also suppose that he not say anything uncomplimentary about BRAND X. What should you conclude about the BRAND X product?

2. Look and listen for examples of the propaganda techniques discussed in this chapter—on TV and radio; in magazines and newspapers, including articles, editorials, letters to the editors, and advertisements; in your school classes; at home;

when you're with your friends; at work; in books and brochures. Which propaganda techniques seem to be used the most?

Problems 3-17: Tell which propaganda techniques are being used in each problem. Ignore faulty reasoning.

3. "The U.S. Marines needs <u>real</u> <u>men</u>! Are you <u>man</u> enough to be a Marine? If you think you are, then see your local recruiter!"

4. "The most popular nightspot in Big City—CROW'S NECK. Come on out to where the action is! Entertainment nightly."

5. Salesman: "Yes, $500 is a lot for a set of books, but you certainly know our company is reliable, and the binding on these books will take many years of heavy use. Wait a minute. I just thought of something. We got orders yesterday from our national headquarters to try to find someone who'd be willing to give personal recommendations to prospects we've lined up, and we were told to sell the set for only $350 to that person. You know how it works—someone might call up and ask how you like your books, and you'd tell him. If you think you're interested, I can talk to our sales manager and see if you could be the one. I can't guarantee anything, because another salesman may already have found someone, but I can certainly take your order on the basis that it's automatically cancelled if you're not the one chosen to give recommendations."

6. "Our present mayor is not doing enough about some of Big City's most serious problems. If you elect me as your mayor, I'll see that there's adequate housing for low income families. I'll see that state and federal funds are obtained to aid us. I'll see that a more enlightened view is taken in the teaching of our kids. I'll make a new effort to enlist top-quality people for our police force."

7. "We're so excited about our new magazine—and so sure that you will be, too—that we'd like to send you the first two issues free. Read them and see how you like them. If you decide you don't want any more issues, simply drop us a line, and that'll be the end of it. Otherwise, we'll add your name to our list of subscribers and bill you $15 for the next 12 issues."

8. "Over 50% of fatal accidents are caused by drunk drivers. We've had highway signs saying, 'Drunk drivers go to jail,' and 'Drunk drivers lose their licenses,' and these have had no effect. Well, I know how to solve the problem. Just impound the car being driven by a drunk. For the first offense, impound it for three months. For the second offense, impound it permanently, and don't allow the driver to buy another car. This way, whether the drunk is driving his own car or someone else's, the car is off the road. People will be very careful about loaning their cars to someone else to drive, and we'll get the drunks off the roads."

9. "Accounting is a good profession. It's interesting work, it pays well, it's respected, you meet interesting people, you're given responsibility, and there are usually good opportunities for advancement."

10. "Don't you think it's strange that her car should go out of control and kill her the day after her husband took out a $100,000 life insurance policy on her? You know, I wondered why he married her in the first place. After all, he's young and good-looking, and she must have been at least 20 years older then he. First I heard that she'd signed over controlling interest in her company as a wedding gift to him, and now this life insurance business comes along. It seems to me that things are starting to add up now, all right!"

11. "Rebecca, if you don't want a spanking, you get yourself inside the house right this minute! And I mean NOW!"

12. Political candidate: "I understand the kinds of problems of every voter in this district, because I grew up in the same circumstances you're in. I was born in a ghetto and lived there until I was eight, so I know what ghetto life is like. My family moved then to a middle-class neighborhood, so I know what the problems of the middle-class people are. My mother won a state lottery when I was fifteen, and we moved again, this time to a rather wealthy neighborhood, so I know about some of the problems of wealthy people. So if you want someone who knows and understands your problems, vote for me!"

13. "I'm Judy Jockey. It was a great thrill for me to win the Kentucky Derby last year. And it was also a great thrill to discover EASY-SADDLE, the saddle padded with foam rubber to make riding more comfortable. Buy an EASY-SADDLE!"

14. "In a study by a leading university, hospital patients with a specific type of pain were sometimes given ASPIRBUFF and were sometimes given just plain aspirin. The study shows that 82% of the patients tested got more relief from ASPIRBUFF than from just plain aspirin. So the next time you get a headache, take ASPIRBUFF."

15. "For a happier home, use CLEAN-ALL! For a healthier home, use CLEAN-ALL! For a prettier home, use CLEAN-ALL!"

16. Telephone caller: "You have been selected to receive free one-year subscriptions to any three magazines you choose from this list: [caller reads the list]. Which magazines would you like to receive?"

17. "This is a nice neighborhood, and I, for one, intend to see that it stays that way! I don't want any no-good kikes moving in! You know how those people like to stick together, and pretty soon we'd have lousy Yids all over the whole neighborhood! You give a kike an inch, and he'll take a mile!"

CHAPTER 6

ADVERTISING AND SCHEMES

6.1   INTRODUCTION

6.2   ''GET RICH QUICK'' SCHEMES

6.3   WHAT'S IN A NAME?

6.4   ADVERTISING SELLS IDEAS

6.5   CAREER OPPORTUNITIES

6.6   STUPID ADVERTISEMENTS

6.7   MISCELLANEOUS SCHEMES

6.8   ASKING QUESTIONS ABOUT ADVERTISEMENTS

6.9   CLASS DISCUSSION PROBLEMS AND QUESTIONS
        FOR CHAPTER REVIEW

6.1 INTRODUCTION

As you learned in chapter 5, many different techniques are used in propaganda. There is much more to learn, however, if you don't want to spend your money foolishly. Even if you learn all the material in this chapter, too, there is no guarantee that you'll always be happy with what you buy. But at least you won't be unhappy as often as you would have been if you hadn't learned this material.

The material included here was selected in the hope that it will give you a good idea of the wide range of schemes which are used and so will make you more careful about parting with your money.

6.2 "GET RICH QUICK" SCHEMES

During your lifetime, you will probably be offered many chances to get rich quick. Some of these offers will be made through advertisements in newspapers or magazines, some will be made by mail, and some will be made in person. As you read about these offers in the following paragraphs and in the problems for this section, remember that the person who makes the offer to you is a professional, not an amateur. He sounds so sincere and so impressive, and he makes the offer sound so plausible, so realistic, so sure-fire, that you have to make a real effort to say "no."

Example 1: Spare-time earnings:

"EARN UP TO $300 A WEEK AT HOME IN YOUR SPARE TIME!"

We'll ignore the fact that "spare time" is not defined. Notice first of all that the ad does not say that you will earn $300 a week—it says you can earn up to $300 a week. It does not promise you that you will earn even $1 a week, regardless of how much time you spend trying. Why not say, "Earn up to $5,000 a week . . ."? Because then no one would believe it, and they want the ad to be believable. So how do you earn this money? Three of the most common ways are these:

a. You send $5 (or whatever) for a list of "proven" ways to earn money at home. (There is no guarantee that you have the knowledge or skills needed to put the ideas into practice, nor is there any guarantee that such knowledge or skill is in demand.)

b. You buy some kind of machine which will allow you to make products "which are in high demand." (Of course, the purpose of the ad in the first place was to sell you the machine, and it's also your problem to sell the products once you make them.)

c. You do telephone calling to try to sell something and you receive a commission on each sale you make. (They could offer you $20 commission on each sale, but if you make only one sale in five hundred calls, you're not earning much for all the time you spend, even if we assume that the telephone calls don't cost you anything extra.)

Example 2: Chain letters:

Someone sends you a letter containing a list of, say, 10 names. The letter contains a warning that it has some kind of mysterious power to bring bad luck to anyone who doesn't do as it says. It tells you to send $1 (or whatever) to the person whose name is at the top of the list and then recopy the letter, leaving out that person's name and including your own name at the bottom of the list, and send the new letter to 10 other people.

Well, why not? After all, you can tell that when your name gets to the top of the list, you're going to make a mint of money. The problem is that the letter would have to circulate to ten billion people before it was time to cross your name off the list. Since there aren't that many people in the whole world, the chances for getting your $1 back don't look too good, do they? Because a great many people have been swindled out of money by this ruse, such chain letters have been declared illegal.

CLASS DISCUSSION PROBLEMS

1. **Foreign prisoner.** You get a letter from someone claiming to be a prisoner in a foreign country. He offers you a share of a secret fortune if you send him money to help him get out of jail. What's wrong?

2. **Heir.** You get a letter or telephone call from someone saying that you may be one of the heirs to an old and valuable estate. The person contacting you says there is a certain amount of legal work and investigating which must be done to verify your claim to the estate. He says he will be willing to do this work on your behalf if you will advance him the necessary expenses and if you agree to share your good fortune—say, 2% of your inheritance—with him. What's wrong?

3. **Animal breeding.** This ad tries to sell you on the idea of breeding animals for profit. Whether it's raising guinea pigs for laboratories, chinchilla or minks for fur, or whatever, the biological statistics given you will be impressive. They may even be mathematically sound, as far as they go. What's wrong?

4. **Tips on the races.** Someone comes up to you and says he has "a hot tip" or "inside information" or "a sure thing" for the next race. He says he's bet all of his own money on it, but he will let you in on it if you'll give him part of your winnings. You agree, and he gives you the name on which you are to bet. You can't lose. You don't pay him anything if the horse loses, and you pay him only part of your winnings if the horse wins. What's wrong?

5. **Pyramid plans.** One of the most common forms of the pyramid plan is to offer you a chance to get "in on the ground floor" of distributing a sensational new product. You are told that you are one of only, say, 10 people in each state being offered this chance. You are to invest $10,000. For every person you can sell on the same deal, you are given $500;

for every person that second person sells on the deal, you are given $100; and for every person that third person sells on the deal, you are given $25. You do some figuring, and you figure that, at the worst, you need to sell the idea to just 20 people to break even. On the other hand, if someone you sell on the deal sells it to one other person who, in turn, sells it to another person, you get $625. On this basis, you need to sell the deal only to 16 people in order to break even. What's wrong?

6. **Oil and gas wells.** Someone offers to sell you an interest in an oil or gas well. He says that geological surveys indicate a high probability of oil or gas, and money is needed to make a mineral-rights agreement with the land owner or to buy well-drilling equipment or to drill deeper. If you will finance 5% (or whatever) of the operation, you'll get 5% of the profit when oil or gas is struck. What's wrong?

6.3 WHAT'S IN A NAME?

What's in a name? Not much, if you think it has to describe the product or service accurately. On the other hand, the name can make the product or service sound very attractive without promising anything. Following are examples of names which make the product or service sound great but which promise nothing.

1. DO-IT-ALL tool
2. CONFIDENTIAL investigation agency
3. ELITE INTERIOR decorators
4. LUXURIOUS carpets
5. DELICIOUS pizza
6. MODERN hair styling
7. EFFICIENT business service
8. MIRACLE wall cleaner
9. BEAUTIFUL COMPLEXION cream
10. FRENCH CHEF salad dressing
11. AVIATOR sunglasses
12. SUPERFAST ice skates

Remember when you see or hear the name of a product, a service, or a company, the name does not necessarily tell you anything about the quality of the thing being sold.

6.4 ADVERTISING SELLS IDEAS

One of the first things you should learn about advertising is that it tries to sell you <u>ideas</u>, not products or services. The advertiser approaches you by telling you about something you'd like to do or be or have, and then he tries to make you think that his product (or service) will give you this something. Or he might approach you by telling you about something you wouldn't like to do or be or have, and he'll try to make you think that his product (or service) will keep you from this something.

Example 1:

"The excitement of Paris! The elegance of the Taj Mahal! The mystery of the Orient! You'll know how devastating you can really be only if you're daring enough to try EXOTIC SCENT!"

You may recognize this as problem 1 in section 5.4. The idea being sold here is that you can be exciting, elegant, mysterious, devastating, and daring. How? By buying EXOTIC SCENT, of course.

Example 2:

"You like dusting every day? Vacuuming the carpet? Cleaning the car upholstery? Wiping the dog's feet when he comes in from a muddy yard? Sweeping the floor? Washing clothes? Washing the walls? Eliminate all of these unpleasant chores with a MIRACLE ELECTRONIC DIRT-REMOVER!"

The idea being sold here is that you don't have to do any of the unpleasant chores named, and you can still live in clean surroundings. All you have to do is buy a MIRACLE ELECTRONIC DIRT-REMOVER.

CLASS DISCUSSION PROBLEMS

In each case, tell what idea the promoter is trying to sell, and tell which, if any, propaganda technique is being used.

1. "Get in the swing of things! Join in the fun! Be someone your friends look forward to seeing! Use NO-SMELL underarm deodorant!"

2. "There's no one else in the world quite like you. That's what makes you so special. And special people deserve the very best. So the next time you color your hair, use GLAMOUR COLOR. It's a little more expensive than other hair coloring products but, after all, you're worth it!"

3. "The softness of kitten fur, the freshness of spring, the radiance of a sunrise. If you want your complexion to be like this, use MAGIC-GLOW COMPLEXION cream."

4. "The astronauts have the most carefully planned, the most nutritionally-balanced meals in history. Nothing but the best for the astronauts, both in nutrition and in quality. And their officially recognized breakfast drink? Not something especially made for them but something you can buy in your local supermarket. SUNSHINE tomato juice! Get SUNSHINE today!"

5. "Feeling tired, run-down, edgy, nervous, irritable lately? You should be the vital, energetic, enthusiastic, smiling, outgoing person you were meant to be! Drink VITAMIX with each meal and see how great you feel!"

6.5 CAREER OPPORTUNITIES

In this section, we'll talk mainly about companies which offer to train you for a new career or offer to test you for your aptitude for a particular career.[1] The approach used may be direct, as in Example 1 below, or it may be indirect, as in Example 2 below.

Example 1:

"Are you putting up with the humdrum monotony of your present job when you could have a stimulating, challenging, respected position as a computer technician? Meet interesting people! Be the person others look to for advice! Call us now for free information about this exciting career opportunity!"

Of course, you should be able to tell that such an ad has been placed by a company who expects you to pay to learn how to be a "computer technician" (whatever that is), not by a company who is ready to hire you and give you free on-the-job training.

Example 2:

"Would you like to join the ranks of famous writers? Send us your autobiography in 500 words or less, and we will send you our opinion of your potential as a writer. This service is absolutely FREE to you! Write to us today!"

What can you lose? It's free, isn't it? Well, the service of giving you an opinion is free, but the ad doesn't say what happens after that.

Ads of the first type may offer you training in any number of careers—for example, hair styling, modeling, keypunch operating, computer programming, or truck driving. In many cases, you will be required to pass some sort of test before signing up for the course "so that you don't waste your money or our time on training for something you're not meant to be." The object may be simply to assure you that you can benefit from such training, thus making you more willing to part with your money. Such tests should not be taken too seriously, since they may be designed so that only morons would fail to "pass" them.

Ads of the second type may offer you opinions of your potential in a number of fields—for example, writing, painting, drawing, dress design, advertising layout, or song-writing. In this case, asking you for a sample of your work may be the promoter's way of making you think that you must have talent if he responds with a favorable opinion of your sample. Let's take a look at a sample autobiography and reply:

Autobiography: "You wanted to no sumthing abowt me so hear goes. I have always want to be a writer ever sence I quit schul in the 3rd grade. My teechurs where always on my back abowt sumthing and I cudunt put up with that nomore nohow so I quit, I bin doing odd jobs ever sence, nuthing fancy."

Reply: "Your writing style is unusual and shows a definite talent for expressing your feelings. Your writing has a natural quality which is not often found in published works. It appears,

---

[1]However, you should also be cautious about ads which offer employment with a shipping company or in a foreign country. Sometimes when you respond to the ad, you're asked to pay $5 (or whatever) for a list of job opportunities, and all you get is a list of American companies having foreign offices or a generalized brochure describing the kinds of jobs done for shipping companies. Of course, the person who placed the ad does not know of any specific job openings right now at all.

124

however, that you may need some guidance about some of the technical points of writing in order to have your writing ready for publication. It may be that your writing problems can be solved in as few as five lessons from our expert staff. We urge you to return the enclosed business reply card to us today so that we can send you your first lesson immediately."

Of course, the business reply card requires some amount to be paid for the lessons.

When you are thinking about signing up for a career-training course, be careful! Such courses may cost over $2,500 and sound great but <u>promise</u> practically nothing! Do some checking on the company which is offering to train you.

Checklist:

1. See if the company is licensed as an educational institution by the state in which it is located. If it is not, find out why.

2. Check with the Better Business Bureau of the city where the company is located. Ask if there have been complaints filed against the company and, if so, what kinds of complaints and what the company did about them.

3. Ask the company for names of former students and for names of businesses which have hired their graduates. Check on the company with these former students and businesses before signing anything.

4. Do some checking on your own with some likely-sounding employers and see if they'd hire a graduate of that company's training program. (Many businesses prefer to do their own training.)

5. Such companies usually offer a "job placement service." Ask what this service includes. Ask what percentage of their graduates have found jobs through them in the past two or three years. Ask for names of businesses who ask them for recommendations, and check with these businesses to verify what you were told.

6. Make sure the company's refund policy is stated clearly. In many cases, you will get no refund regardless of whether or not you complete the course or are satisfied with it.

7. **Read the contract before you sign it.** In most cases, the contract will have a statement such as, "The Company is responsible only for the terms and conditions stated in this contract and is not responsible for any representations to the contrary which may have been made by any of its employees or agents."[1]

And don't let yourself be high-pressured into signing up for the course before you've checked on the company offering it!

---

[1]Don't confuse what the salesman told you with what the contract tells you. Suppose the contract says there are no refunds after the first week of class, and the salesman tells you, "That's just in the contract to protect us from the crackpot who signs up with no intention of working to learn, and then he tries to get out of the contract. If you were to become ill, or move out of the area, or get a job with hours so that you couldn't attend classes any longer, you'd get a refund." You'll probably find out to your sorrow that the contract meant what it said—no refunds, and the Company is not responsible for what a salesman may have told you.

6.6 STUPID ADVERTISEMENTS

It's one thing for an advertisement to be stupid in the sense that it's funny and is meant to be funny. It's a different thing for it to be stupid in the sense that it's unintelligent and is meant to be taken seriously. In this section, you'll find some ads which I believe fall into the second category.[1]

Example 1:

A TV ad shows a lovely green-skinned girl bouncing along in the sun. She is obviously happy as she says, "Until someone told me about PERFECT GREEN, I didn't want to dye my skin. You know how some of these products are—they streak, or they're messy, or you can never be sure of the results. But look how terrific my skin looks after using PERFECT GREEN! Now your skin can look like this! Do it! There's no excuse not to!"

Even if we believe what the girl says, so what? There may be a reason not to do it. And even if there isn't a reason not to do it, is there a reason to do it?

Example 2:

"Come to us for a real bargain price! If we can't sell it at the lowest possible price, then we won't sell it at all!"

You may recognize this as problem 5 in section 5.8. The second sentence, of course, is saying, "If we can't sell it, then we won't sell it." That figures.

CLASS DISCUSSION PROBLEMS

Pretend you're a mind reader, and try to figure out why I think each of the following advertisements is stupid.

1. "Every single appliance—every single brand name, every single color, every single model—is sale-priced 365 days a year!"

2. "More doctors recommend CANCERETTE cigarettes to patients who smoke cigarettes than any other brand."

3. "I'm no authority on the subject, so if I told you, you might not believe it. But what if I said that there's scientific evidence that said flying saucers using FLASH-RITE lights have fewer breakdowns?"

4. "And now, here's this week's no-nonsense special at a price so low you just won't believe it!"

5. A TV ad shows a girl shopping for an expensive dress. She says, "Oh, Sis, do you think Bernie will like me in this?" Sis stands next to the girl and answers, "Honey, you don't need something expensive like that to impress Bernie. Do as I do. Put your money where your mouth is, and buy SPARKLE mouthwash. Fresh breath is what'll impress him." The girl asks, "Does SPARKLE mouthwash make your breath fresh?" Sis answers, smiling, "As fresh as it can be."

6. "If my kids like SOAPY soap, they might wash longer!"

7. "Buy a CLEAR-PIC TV set now! Nobody in the world can make the offer being made to you by CLEAR-PIC!"

---

[1] The products and brand names have been changed to protect my publisher and me from lawsuits, however.

6.7 MISCELLANEOUS SCHEMES

There are many schemes to get you to part with your money, some of which you've already learned about in sections 6.2 and 6.5. The schemes listed below will give you a better idea of the wide variety of schemes used, but you should realize that these represent only a fraction of possible schemes.

Puzzle Contests: The ad tells you to complete the puzzle and send it, along with 50¢ entry fee, in order to enter a contest offering a $100,000 grand prize. The puzzle says, "Fill in the blanks so that the words name a well-known President of the United States: G _ O R G _ W _ S H _ N G T _ N."

The catch is that there are a whole series of puzzles to complete, each of which is more difficult than the preceding one, and each of which you must return with money in order to stay in the contest. The last few puzzles are extremely hard.

Display Photo: After placing an order for photographs you had taken at a studio, you receive a letter saying, "Your portrait has been selected for display at our studio. It will be in our living color, silk-screen-process, radiant tone velvet finish and will have a retail value of $50. In consideration of your allowing us to use it for display purposes, however, you may have it for only $25 when we are through displaying it."

They're trying to sell you another photograph, of course, and are trying to make you think you'll be getting a bargain if you buy it.

Photo Contest: You are told that a modeling agency or a TV studio is looking for new faces and that they will make their initial selections from photographs. It is pointed out that the competition will be stiff and that you'll have a much better chance of winning, of course, if you submit a photograph taken by a professional photographer.

This is probably just another way to get business for a photographer. Ask for the name of the modeling agency or TV studio and then telephone or write to check out the information you were given.

Photo Certificate: You are shown a sample photograph from X STUDIO and given a certificate saying that you can get an X STUDIO photograph of yourself for only $2 (or whatever).

You may run into two difficulties here: first, you may have to order a certain number of pictures at the regular price before you can use your certificate; second, the quality of your photograph may not be as good as the sample you were shown.

Prize Certificate: You are awarded a contest prize of a certificate which is good toward the cost of merchandise.

Watch out for these. The merchandise may be of inferior quality, and the price may be overstated by enough to make up for the certificate. Thus, you may "win" a certificate worth $50 toward the $275 price of a new sewing machine, when the sewing machine is worth only about $200 in the first place.

Inspector: Someone comes to your house and says he is a furnace inspector. He may tear down your furnace and tell you it is dangerous and cannot be repaired.

The man may be nothing more than a salesman for a furnace company who will give you bad news about your furnace whether or not your furnace is good. Always check the identification papers of such a person and call your city offices to check his story <u>before</u> you allow him to examine your furnace. (Another version of this scheme is the "termite inspector" who tells you that your house is infested with termites and needs extensive repairs.)

Landscaping: You may be told that sod, shrubs, trees, or flowers are of high quality and then find after you buy them that they are of very low quality.

Know the company you're dealing with. If sod and young trees and shrubs are of good quality, then they are usually expensive, and most honest nurseries and landscapers will give you a reasonable guarantee on the stock you buy from them.

Model Home: A salesman quotes you a price on some kind of home improvement job (for example, paving a driveway, installing awnings or aluminum siding, landscaping, fencing, building a garage) and then says his company has been looking for a home to use as a model in your neighborhood. He says you'll get a discount—say, 25%—if you'll agree to let them bring other people around to see the good job they did on your house.

Do you recognize this scheme as another version of "Prize Certificate"? Always get two or three estimates on the job you want done, and insist that the quality of material to be used be stated on the estimate.

Neighborhood: Some workmen with a truck stop at your house and tell you they just finished a job down the street (surfacing a driveway, repairing a roof or a chimney, waterproofing a basement, or whatever). They say they ordered too much material for the job, and they offer to do a job for you at cost so that they don't have to take a loss on the material.

This is a favorite scheme used by crooked operators in older sections of a city. Both the material and the workmanship may be inferior, and the price you pay is often more than it would have cost to have a good job done.

Unordered Merchandise: You receive unordered merchandise in the mail, probably accompanied by an appeal for a donation to some charitable cause.

The charitable cause may or may not be faked. Under present laws, you are not legally required either to pay for the merchandise or to return it.

List Price: The salesman shows you the manufacturer's list price or recommended selling price on a product and he says he'll sell you the product for less than that.

In a good-sized city, most things are sold below the list prices these days, whether it's a $5,000 new car or a $20 food blender, so you shouldn't think that you're getting a "good deal" just because you'll pay less than the list price.

"Factory gate" selling: Jewelry or other merchandise may be offered for sale at a location near a factory or office entrance. The brand names may look familiar, and the fast-talking salesman assures you that the prices are low because he doesn't have to pay for the overhead of an office and a staff to run it. He urges you to try out the merchandise for a few days and just sign a receipt for it in the meantime.

The "receipt" you sign may turn out to be a binding contract to pay for the merchandise whether or not you decide you want to keep it. Furthermore, the brand names may look familiar because they are deliberately close to well-known brand names—for example, "Longenes" instead of "Longines," or "Westinhouse" instead of "Westinghouse."

Summary:
1. Don't let yourself be high-pressured into buying something. Salesmen know that people who are enthused over something right now may not be enthused when they've thought it over a while.
2. Don't expect high-quality merchandise for a low-quality price.
3. Be suspicious of "a good deal." Ask yourself, "And what's the catch?"
4. Make sure the person or company you're dealing with has a good reputation.
5. Don't buy anything until you find out what its usual selling price is, and check on this yourself—don't take the salesman's word for it.

6.8 ASKING QUESTIONS ABOUT ADVERTISEMENTS

Asking questions is one of your best defenses against spending your money foolishly. We know that science and research are continually making new and better products available, and this makes it easy to think that an advertisement promised something which was not promised at all. Before you rush out and buy a product you've seen advertised, look and listen carefully to what the ad really says.

CLASS DISCUSSION PROBLEMS

1. The TV announcer shows us five identical bowls containing clear liquid. He has an eyedropper full of something black and goes to each bowl in turn, placing a drop of black fluid in each bowl of solution. He says as he goes along, "This eyedropper contains grease, and each bowl contains a solution of one of five leading laundry detergents. We're placing a drop of grease in each bowl. Nothing happens in bowl no. 1—the grease just floats on top. Nothing happens in bowl no. 2, no. 3, no. 4. But look in bowl no. 5! The grease is breaking up! And this is the bowl containing the SUDSO detergent solution!" Assume the announcer is telling the truth.

   (1) There were five bowls and five solutions shown. How many detergents were used to make up these five solutions?

(2) Were each of the five solutions of equal strength? For example, if bowl no. 5 contained a tablespoon of SUDSO and a cup of water, did the other bowls also contain a tablespoon of detergent and a cup of water?

(3) Was the water temperature in bowl no. 5 the same as in the other four bowls?

(4) Was the same kind of water (hard, soft, water from the same tap) used in all five bowls?

(5) Did bowl no. 5 contain additional laundry aids not in the other bowls—for example, water softener or a special chemical to dissolve grease?

(6) a. How long did it take the solution in bowl no. 5 to break up the grease?
   b. Did we see what happened to the other grease drops after this same amount of time?

(7) Suppose the test was a fair one—all bowls contained the same solution strength, water temperature, etc., and only the detergent brands were different. Now think about what a laundry detergent should do and give a reason for wanting to have the results in bowls no. 1-4 and not wanting the result in bowl no. 5.

2. The woman on TV says, "I'm Mrs. Nina Nobody. My husband is an auto mechanic, and his clothes get full of grease, oil, and dirt from his work. I used to dread washing clothes, but then I discovered SUDSO. [Movie shows filthy work clothes being put into washer, clean work clothes being taken out.] Now I just toss my husband's work clothes in with some SUDSO and they come out clean." Assume the woman is telling the truth.

(1) How many times must the clothes be washed in order to get them clean?

(2) Does Mrs. Nobody still dread washing clothes?

(3) Did the product Mrs. Nobody used to use also get her her husband's work clothes clean?

(4) Does SUDSO get Mr. Nobody's work clothes clean?

(5) How long does Mrs. Nobody let the dirty clothes lie around before washing them?

(6) What kind of water does Mrs. Nobody use for washing clothes (hard, soft)?

(7) Does Mrs. Nobody use any product besides SUDSO when washing the work clothes?

(8) What's the point of asking questions (5)-(7)?

(9) If you had clothes full of grease, oil, and dirt, would SUDSO get them clean?

3. "In studies conducted by two universities on pain other than headache, PAINOUT worked better than aspirin. So when you have pain, don't bother with aspirin—take PAINOUT."

(1) Which universities made the studies?

(2) Which colleges within the universities made the studies?

(3) How many studies were made?

(4) a. How many people were tested in each study?
   b. How many people were tested in all of the studies combined?

(5) What process was used to select the people to be tested?

(6) Did the "PAINOUT" people and the "aspirin" people know what they were being given for their pain?

(7) What kind of pain was tested in the study?

(8) Were remedies other than PAINOUT and aspirin also tried? If so, what were the results?

(9) What is meant by "worked better than" in the advertisement?

(10) What is the probability that the results would be the same for an average person having the same kind of pain as in the studies?

(11) If you have pain, would PAINOUT work better than aspirin for you?

(12) Suppose you were one of the people tested, and suppose PAINOUT worked better for you than aspirin. If you have pain now, would PAINOUT probably work better for you than aspirin?

4. "Are you putting up with the humdrum monotony of your present job when you could have a stimulating, challenging, respected position as a computer technician? Meet interesting people! Be the person others look to for advice! Call us now for free information about this exciting career opportunity!"

(1) Does the ad say that you could have a position as a computer technician?

(2) Does the ad say that being a computer technician is an exciting career?

(3) Does the ad say that you will meet interesting people if you
   a. call for free information?
   b. become a computer technician?

(4) Does the ad say that other people will look to you for advice if you
   a. call for free information?
   b. become a computer technician?

(5) Does the ad say that all computer technicians find their positions stimulating, challenging, and respected?

(6) Does the ad imply that you are being asked to apply for an available position as a computer technician?

(7) Does the ad imply that you can learn to be a computer technician at no cost to yourself?

(8) What's a computer technician?

131

6.9 CLASS DISCUSSION PROBLEMS AND QUESTIONS FOR CHAPTER REVIEW

1. Your eight-year-old car is in pretty bad shape, and you've been thinking about getting a new car, but you can't afford it. You park your car in a parking lot, and when you come back, there is a note on the windshield: "I have a buyer for your car. Would you take $1,550 for it as a trade-in on a new SUPER-8? We must act right away. Call or bring in your car today." The telephone number and address are also on the note. What's wrong?

2. You go shopping for a used car and find one you like, but you have to have it financed. The salesman tells you the finance charge is only 6%. What's wrong?

3. You don't know a lot about cars, but you need one and so you shop for a used car. You find one you like: the body and tires look good; it's clean inside; you take it for a test drive and it sounds good. Why shouldn't you buy it yet?

4. You get a letter offering you what seems to be a really good deal in insurance—broad coverage, low rates. What's wrong?

5. "You can't protect your baby entirely from the world of germs. But you can sure try. Use KILGERM on the things your baby touches—crib, clothes, toys, bathtub, stroller, bottles, blankets. Keep your baby happy and healthy! Get KILGERM today!"
   (1) What idea is being sold in this ad?
   (2) Is the first statement of the ad true?
   (3) If a baby is normal, should its parents try to protect it entirely from the world of germs? Why?
   (4) Does the ad say that your baby will be happy and healthy if you use KILGERM?
   (5) Does the ad say that your baby will be happier and healthier if you use KILGERM than if you don't use KILGERM?

6. "There's no one else in the world quite like you. That's what makes you so special. And special people deserve the very best. So the next time you color your hair, use GLAMOUR-COLOR. It's a little more expensive than other hair coloring products but, after all, you're worth it!"
   (1) Is the first statement of the ad true?
   (2) Is the third statement of the ad true? Why?
   For questions (3)-(5) below, accept the statements in the ad as true.
   (3) Is GLAMOUR-COLOR a better hair coloring product than other brands?
   (4) Is GLAMOUR-COLOR a more expensive hair coloring product than other brands?
   (5) According to the ad, why should you be willing to pay more for GLAMOUR-COLOR than for other brands?

7. "Feeling tired, run-down, edgy, nervous, irritable lately? You should be the vital, energetic, enthusiastic, smiling, outgoing person you were meant to be! Drink VITAMIX with each meal and see how great you feel!"
   (1) Is the second sentence of the ad true? Why?

(2) Does the ad say that if you drink VITAMIX with each meal you'll be vital? energetic? enthusiastic? smiling? outgoing?

(3) Does the ad say that if you drink VITAMIX with each meal, you won't feel tired? run-down? edgy? nervous? irritable?

(4) Does the ad say that if you drink VITAMIX with each meal, you'll feel great?

8. "The softness of kitten fur, the freshness of spring, the radiance of a sunrise. If you want your complexion to be like this, use MAGIC-GLOW COMPLEXION cream." Assume the ad is telling the truth.

(1) At what general group is this ad directed?

(2) Will MAGIC-GLOW COMPLEXION cream make your complexion
   a. as soft as kitten fur?
   b. as fresh as spring?
   c. as radiant as a sunrise?

(3) Does the ad say that your complexion will be soft, fresh, and radiant if you use MAGIC-GLOW COMPLEXION cream?

9. "DO YOU WANT A CLEAN bathroom? USE MAGIC-KLEEN!
DO YOU WANT A CLEAN basement? USE MAGIC-KLEEN!
DO YOU WANT A CLEAN sidewalk? USE MAGIC-KLEEN!
DO YOU WANT A CLEAN kitchen? USE MAGIC-KLEEN!
DO YOU WANT A CLEAN garage? USE MAGIC-KLEEN!"

(1) Does the ad say that MAGIC-KLEEN works like magic?

(2) Does the ad say that if you use MAGIC-KLEEN on your
   _____, it will be clean?
   (a) bathroom?
   (b) basement?
   (c) sidewalk?
   (d) kitchen?
   (e) garage?

10. "My opponent said he would work for better housing. But he voted against the Fair-Housing Bill. My opponent said he would work for better schools. But he voted against Bill No. 47, which granted federal aid to schools. My opponent said he would work for safer cities. But he voted against Bill No. 204 to provide federal aid to cities wishing to update their training of police officers."

Assume the speaker is telling the truth. Call his opponent "X."

(1) Why did X vote against the Fair-Housing Bill?

(2) Is it possible that X thought that the Fair-Housing Bill was poor and that he had already introduced a much better housing bill?

(3) Why did X vote against Bill No. 47?

(4) Is it possible that X thought that Bill No. 47 did not offer enough aid to schools and that if it were defeated, a bill offering more aid would be passed?

(5) Why did X vote against Bill No. 204?

(6) If X was working for safer cities, then why might he have voted against Bill No. 204?

11. The announcer says, "What do you think about SPRAY-ON rug shampoo, Arnie?" Arnaldo Astronaut, Spain's famous astronaut, says, "I think SPRAY-ON is the best rug shampoo I've ever used. I think everyone should try it."
Assume that Arnie is telling the truth.

    (1) How many other rug shampoos has Arnie used?

    (2) Does Arnie think that SPRAY-ON is a good rug shampoo?

    (3) How much does Arnie know about what a rug shampoo should and should not do?

12. "Let us send the FORCE SCREEN MACHINE to you for a free 10-day trial. Use it as much as you like for 10 full days, and if you're not absolutely delighted with it, just return it to us undamaged, postage prepaid, at the end of the 10 days and owe us nothing. Orders will be filled according to their postmarks, and we can't guarantee how long the FORCE SCREEN MACHINE will be available, so send us your order TODAY!"
Suppose the cost of the FORCE SCREEN MACHINE is $998. What else would you want to know before you sent for it on a 10-day trial basis?

13. Go back to problem 5 in section 5.12. The approach used in this problem is similar to what scheme in section 6.7?

CHAPTER 7

EXAMINING ARGUMENTS AND VALUE JUDGMENTS

7.1   RULES OF A SOCIETY

7.2   PROTECTION OF THE LAW

7.3   EMOTIONAL WORDS AND ARGUMENTS

7.4   DOUBLE STANDARDS

7.5   WHERE DO YOU DRAW THE LINE?

7.6   ATTRIBUTES OF A GOOD ARGUMENT

7.7   CLASS DISCUSSION PROBLEMS AND QUESTIONS
        FOR CHAPTER REVIEW

7.1 RULES OF A SOCIETY

Any society, whether primitive or advanced, has certain rules to be followed. Punishment for breaking a rule may be merely a frown (if the rule is about a minor matter) or it may be death (if the rule is about a major matter).

Someone in a society may not believe that all of the rules are important. Then he has two basic choices: he can live as though the rules don't exist, or he can obey the rules because he doesn't want his fellow citizens to think unkindly of him. He may follow the path of convenience: when he's around someone he wants to think well of him, he follows the rules; when he's around someone and doesn't care what the other person thinks of him, he doesn't follow the rules.

Or someone may think that the rules apply to other people but not to himself. (Do you recognize the special pleading here?) Then he expects to enjoy the privileges, but not to assume the responsibilities, which go with the rules: he expects other people to treat him according to the rules, but he doesn't think he should have to treat other people according to the rules.

CLASS DISCUSSION PROBLEMS

1. Why does a society have rules?
2. List ten rules your society has.
3. List any rules your society has which you believe should not be followed. Explain.
4. List any rules your society has which you believe are unimportant in the sense that it doesn't matter one way or another whether or not they are followed. Explain.
5. You've probably heard someone object to a rule, saying, "You should be allowed to do anything you want to do, as long as you're not hurting anyone else by doing it."
   a. Do you agree with that person's statement? Why?
   b. If your answer to "a" is "yes," describe at least one situation in which the person should be allowed to do as he wishes, even though there is a rule against it.

7.2 PROTECTION OF THE LAW

There is a big difference between assuming that a man is guilty until he is proved innocent, and assuming a man is innocent until he is proved guilty. In the United States, of course, we assume a man is innocent until he is proved guilty.

If you're on a jury, you're not necessarily supposed to believe that the accused person is innocent if you vote "not guilty." All you need for a "not guilty" vote is a reasonable doubt of his guilt.

This doesn't mean that just any doubt will do. For example, it may be possible that an accused person is telling the truth when he says, "There I was, just minding my own business, and along comes this giant 2000-pound canary. It picks me up and carries me right to the murder scene. I'm standing there scared as anything when the police walk in and say I'm a murderer. And then just as the police look toward the canary, it vanishes into thin air." But such a story should not give you a reasonable doubt of the suspect's guilt.

The assumption that we are innocent until proved guilty beyond a reasonable doubt is one way our laws protect us. Another way is in the U.S. Supreme Court decision that a conviction may be reversed if the police do not tell us our rights before they question us:

> You have the right to remain silent. Anything you say can and will be used against you in a court of law. You have the right to talk to a lawyer before answering any questions. You have the right to have a lawyer present with you while you are answering any questions. If you cannot afford to hire a lawyer, one will be appointed to represent you before any questioning if you wish one. You have the right to decide at any time before or during questioning to use your right to remain silent and your right to a lawyer while you are being questioned.

The police then follow this information with questions such as, "Do you understand each of the rights I have told you?" "Do you want to talk to a lawyer before being questioned?" "Do you waive your right to remain silent?"

Such provisions of the law protect not only the innocent, of course, but the guilty as well. They seem to be the American way of answering the question, "Which is worse—to let a crime go unpunished, or to punish someone for a crime he did not commit?"

CLASS DISCUSSION PROBLEMS

1. This section describes two ways in which the law protects you. List or describe at least five other ways in which the law protects you. If you prefer, list at least five laws which protect you.
2. State or describe at least one law which may be inconvenient to obey at times but which protects the rights or safety of other people.
3. You have probably read or heard of criminals who have gone free because of a technicality in the law. Do you think this should be allowed to happen? Why?
4. Which do you think is worse—to let a crime go unpunished, or to punish someone for a crime he did not commit? Why?
5. One of the statements in this section says that a lawyer will be appointed to represent you during questioning if you can't afford to hire one and wish to have one.
   a. Who pays for this lawyer?

137

b. Who appoints the lawyer?

c. Trials cost the taxpayers a good deal of money. Why should honest taxpayers have to pay for the trial of a criminal?

6. Following is a letter to the editor of a newspaper:

To the Editor: Americans should wake up to the disease which is ruining us. There has always been crime and corruption, but it isn't necessary to let it engulf us.

We are being assaulted openly by traitors. Members of the X-GROUP in particular should be rounded up and tried for treason. People who bomb and kill and stir up riots should be tried in court and then shot or banished from America.

This is not their country if they won't help build it!

(1) Does the writer appear to be pleased, or displeased? About what?

(2) The first sentence of the letter talks about disease. To what disease does it refer?

(3) Do you agree with the second sentence of the letter? Why?

(4) The writer makes a serious charge in his third sentence. Where is this backed up in the letter?

(5) The writer wants members of the X-GROUP tried for treason. Why?

(6) Read the next-to-last sentence carefully. What's wrong with the reasoning here?

(7) Do you agree with the last sentence of the letter? Why?

(8) Go back to the second sentence of the letter. How does the writer propose to keep us from being engulfed by crime and corruption?

(9) The writer says, "We are being assaulted openly by traitors." What does he propose as a remedy?

(10) Does the writer appear to believe that

a. American citizens are letting criminals get away with too much?

b. America is worth trying to save from crime, corruption, and traitors?

(11) What is your overall reaction to the writer's letter? (Has he proposed good solutions to the problems he lists? Is his reasoning good?)

(12) Does the writer appear to believe that the end justifies the means?

7. Following is a letter to the editor of a newspaper:

To the Editor: We will never have peace unless Communism is erased from the face of the earth. There are thousands of Communists in our country, many of who are disguised.

Communists are on our college campuses, where there are riots, and in every part of the world of entertainment. They expel their loathsome filth wherever they can.

I resent our nation being called sick. The only sick ones are those who preach communistic tactics and the ones who listen and follow suit.

We should stop all entry into the United States. Then we should go on a weeding party and deport all undesirables without a court hearing. Then we should enforce stronger immigration laws before letting anyone enter this country again.

(1) Does the writer appear to be pleased, or displeased? About what?

(2) In the second sentence of the second paragraph, what does the writer mean by "loathsome filth"?

(3) How does the writer back up
   a. his first sentence?
   b. the first part of his second sentence?
   c. the second part of his second sentence?
   d. the second sentence of the second paragraph?

(4) Why does the writer resent our nation's being called sick?

(5) Do you agree with the second sentence of the third paragraph? Explain.

(6) In the last paragraph, what does the writer mean when he says, "We should go on a weeding party"?

(7) Who all does the writer intend to include when he says "all undesirables" in the last paragraph?

(8) a. How does the writer suggest we locate people who may be "undesirables"?
   b. How does the writer suggest we go about deciding whether or not people are "undesirables"?
   c. Why does the writer want to deport all undesirables without a court hearing?

(9) Give an example of what the writer means by "stronger immigration laws."

(10) Is the writer in favor of the American system of justice?

(11) Find an example of special pleading in this letter.

(12) a. Do you think the writer states a good argument for deporting communists from the United States?
   b. Read the letter again, but this time substitute "motherhood" for "communism" and "communistic," and substitute "mothers" for "communists." Do you think the writer states a good argument for deporting mothers from the United States?
   c. If your answers to "a" and "b" are not the same, explain why.

(13) Suppose it were possible to round up and deport all communists from the United States. Would you be in favor of such action? Why?

7.3 EMOTIONAL WORDS AND ARGUMENTS

We will say that an argument is an emotional argument if it is based mostly on, or if it appeals mostly to, emotions rather than logic. You learned about one kind of emotional argument, "name-calling," in section 5.10. Another emotional argument is given in problem 6 of section 5.6. Still others are given in problems 6 and 7 of section 7.2.

Some words or phrases may be either emotional or unemotional, depending on how we use them.

Example 1:

Unemotional: "Our city trash collectors are good men. If we happen to leave something outside which still looks good, they don't pick it up. They pick up nothing but trash."

Emotional: "That book is nothing but trash!"

Also, we can express the same basic idea but give it different shades of meaning by our choice of words. In special pleading, different words may be used to describe the same thing and have quite different suggested meanings.

Example 2:

"I complimented the boss. You flattered him. That guy over there laid it on pretty thick."

All three statements mean that something nice was said, but they have different suggested meanings: "complimented" suggests that something good was recognized and remarked about; "flattered" suggests that the remark made the good thing sound better than it really was; "laid it on pretty thick" suggests that the "good" thing was made to sound "fantastic" by the remark.

Many of our words and expressions are primarily emotional. For example, describing someone as "a tough guy," "stuck-up," or "creepy" is an emotional description. Or saying that someone "is out to get you" or "has it in for you" or "double-crossed" you or "covered up" for you is an emotional description.

Example 3:

Neutral: "Mr. Jorger tells me a lot to stop talking."

Emotional: "Mr. Jorger is always picking on me."

Emotional arguments are often, but not always, poor arguments. Problems 6 and 7 in section 7.2 are examples of poor emotional arguments, but problem 6 in section 5.6 is an example of a good emotional argument.

CLASS DISCUSSION PROBLEMS

1. Is an emotional argument always a poor argument?
2. Is a poor argument always an emotional argument?

Problems 3-8: Restate each problem so that only neutral words and phrases are used and so that the same meaning is kept.

3. "He thinks he's another Einstein."
4. "She's nosy."
5. "He really raked me over the coals."

6. "She swallowed the story hook, line, and sinker."
7. "He's a snake in the grass."
8. "She's pigheaded."

9. "To the Editor: Some of us don't have jobs, and instead of doing something about it, the government sits on its hands and feeds us garbage about things working themselves out. The founding fathers of our once great country would hang their heads in shame if they could see the way the government takes money for milk from hungry babies and shoots it into outer space. What good is a government that won't take care of its citizens?"

(1) In the second paragraph of this section, it was said that an expression may be either emotional or unemotional, depending on how it is used. Decide which of the following expressions seem to have been used emotionally in the letter.
   a. jobs
   b. government
   c. sits on its hands
   d. feeds us garbage
   e. founding fathers of our once great country
   f. hang their heads in shame
   g. takes money for milk from hungry babies
   h. shoots money into outer space

(2) In answering the questions which follow, don't worry about whether or not the writer actually said the things you are asked about. Answer the questions on the basis of how he seems to think according to what he said in the letter.
Does the writer seem to think that
   a. the government should do something about getting jobs for people who don't have jobs?
   b. the government does not tell us the truth?
   c. the government is not doing the things for its citizens which our founding fathers intended it to do?
   d. the government does not care whether or not babies go hungry?
   e. the government cares more about exploring outer space than about feeding hungry babies?
   f. our country is no longer great?
   g. the government does not take care of its citizens?
   h. our government is no good?

(3) The writer is obviously unhappy about some things. What suggestions does he give to make the situations better?

(4) According to the question he asks, the writer seems to feel that the government should take care of its citizens.
   a. How far does he seem to think the government should go in taking care of its citizens?
   b. Do you agree that the government should go that far in taking care of its citizens? Explain.

10. "To the Editor: It makes me sick to my stomach to see what's going on today. As fast as our police catch juvenile delinquents, our bleeding-heart judges let these young punks out on probation, free to roam the streets in search of new prey. Don't give me any of that rot about, "It's not their fault. They weren't given a decent childhood." Every human being is responsible for his own actions starting at the age of seven. If these hoodlums don't want to obey the laws of the society around them, then they should be taken out of that society, not set free to break the laws again and again and cause the rest of us to live in fear, each wondering if he'll be the next victim of one of these teen-aged monsters."

   (1) List the emotional expressions used in this letter.

   (2) a. About what is the letter writer displeased?

       b. Are you displeased about this situation, too? Why?

   (3) a. What does the writer suggest in order to make the situation better?

       b. Do you think that his suggestion is a good one? Why?

       c. If your answer to "b" was "no," what do you think should be done instead?

7.4 DOUBLE STANDARDS

A **double standard** is a rule of society which is applied more strictly to one group of people than to another, or which is applied more strictly under some circumstances than under others. Someone who uses a double standard is also using special pleading.

Example 1:

In the early days of U.S. history, white men who fought Indians were called "heroes," but Indians who fought white men were called "savages."

Example 2:

Some parents think that when a teacher yells at someone else's kid, the kid probably had it coming; but when the teacher yells at their own kid, the teacher is picking on him.

Example 3:

Some people think that it's OK for a husband to go to work and support his wife while she stays home and takes care of the house, but it isn't OK for a wife to go to work and support her husband while he stays home and takes care of the house.

Example 4:

Some people think it's OK to steal from someone you don't know, but it's not OK to steal from someone you know.

Example 5:

Some people think that if someone of their own race drives a luxury car, that's OK; but if someone of another race drives a luxury car, he's "just trying to show off."

As you can tell from the examples above, there is no question that double standards exist in our society. The question you must answer for yourself is, "If it's right sometimes, then why isn't it right all the time?" or, "If it's wrong sometimes, then why isn't it wrong all the time?"

CLASS DISCUSSION PROBLEMS

1. Give three examples (not in the textbook) of double standards.
2. Someone once said, "Standards are good to have. Therefore, double standards are twice as good." What's wrong with this reasoning?
3. In a letter to the editor of Big City's newspaper, someone wrote, "A white mayor advocating the need for the return of white families to Big City would be called a racist. But a black mayor would not." Did the writer give an example of a double standard? Explain.
4. "To the Editor: Your moral indignation at the way the governments of other countries ignore their poverty-stricken citizens has a hollow ring. Where is your moral indignation about the living conditions of the American Indians and of the people living in the slum sections of every big city in America? In your moral outlook, what is left undone is not as important as who is leaving it undone."
   a. Is the writer accusing the editor of using a double standard? Explain.
   b. Do you think the editor is using a double standard? Why?

5. **"EVERYBODY DOES IT"**

   When Anthony was four years old, he broke a playmate's toy on purpose. His mother lied to the playmate's parents, telling them that Anthony cut his hand on the toy and could have been badly hurt. She told them she certainly was not going to pay for the toy and that they were lucky they didn't get sued for allowing Anthony to play with such a dangerous toy. "It's all right, baby," she told Anthony. "Everybody does it."

   When Anthony was seven, his dad brought home some paneling for the den from the construction company where he worked. "No, I didn't pay for it, but that's OK," his dad said. "Everybody does it."

   When Anthony was ten, his uncle was umpiring at home plate in a Little League ball game. When Anthony was up at bat, his uncle called four balls in a row, and three of the calls should have been strikes. His uncle winked at him and said, "It's OK, kid. Everybody does it."

   When Anthony was thirteen, he needed a book report in a hurry. His aunt showed him one she'd written as a high school student and said he could copy it and turn it in. "It's OK, Tony," she said. "Everyone does it."

   When he was sixteen, Anthony entered a science fair project and purposely failed to acknowledge all the help he had received on it from various people. "It's OK, man," his brother told him. "Everybody does it."

When Anthony was nineteen and a freshman in college, a senior offered to sell him the answers to three exams. "It's OK, frosh," he said. "Everybody does it." So Anthony bought the answers. He and the senior were caught, exposed publicly, and expelled from college.

"How could you disgrace us like that?!" his mother cried.

"You've shamed your whole family," his father said sadly.

"I don't understand how you could do a thing like that," his uncle said.

"You've been raised to know better than to do something like that!" his aunt exclaimed.

"I'm really disappointed in you, Tony," his brother said. "You've let us all down."

"The youth of today have no sense of moral standards," said the psychiatrist. "They can't distinguish between right and wrong."

"The youth of today have alarmingly weak characters," said the sociologist.

"Well, we got rid of those rotten good-for-nothings," said the dean of the college. "Now we can hold our heads high again."

If there's anything an adult can't stand, it's a kid who cheats.

(1) Who used a double standard in the story?

(2) What excuse did Anthony's mother give him for lying to the playmate's parents?

(3) What excuse did Anthony's father give him for stealing from the company?

(4) What excuse did Anthony's uncle give him for cheating at baseball?

(5) What excuse did Anthony's aunt give him for cheating on a book report?

(6) What excuse did Anthony's brother give him for being dishonest about a science fair project?

(7) What did Anthony do to make his relatives so upset with him?

6. Following is an article from Big City's newspaper:

**PENALTY TOO SEVERE,
EX-SUPER-8 EXECUTIVES FEEL**

"People used to tell me I must have small SUPER-8's instead of blood running up and down my veins. That's how much I thought of them," said Martin Zarward, who worked for SUPER-8 Company for 23 years until they fired him last March.

Zarward was one of over 35 employees fired by the SUPER-8 Company on March 8th and 9th in a two-day shakeup of its Big City regional offices. The company has refused to talk about the reasons for the firings, other than to verify that the ousted employees had directly violated a written company policy which prohibits employees from accepting gifts from SUPER-8 customers and suppliers.

Zarward's discharge left him angry and upset. "I'm not angry at the company," he said. "I still think SUPER-8 is the best car made. I'm angry at the people who thought up this plot to embarrass all of us they fired." While readily acknowledging that what he did was in violation of the company's written policy, he said such disregard of the policy was a common practice among employees at the Big City office. "I think firing us was too extreme," he said. "They should have at least warned us first."

Gerald Balenge, another SUPER-8 Company executive in Big City who was fired in the shakeup, admitted that he knew about the policy when he was hired and that he received over $500 last year in gift certificates from SUPER-8 Company suppliers and customers, in addition to receiving a month's free use of vacation facilities owned by one of the suppliers. "I wouldn't have done it if I'd known the company was going to fire me for it," he said. "SUPER-8's executives all over the country do this. I feel that we have been singled out unfairly in order to make an example of us."

Assuming that the newspaper is telling the truth, answer the following questions.

(1) Does Zarward profess to be loyal to the SUPER-8 Company?

(2) Did Zarward know he was violating a company policy when he violated it?

(3) What reason did Zarward give for violating the company's policy?

(4) In the third paragraph, Zarward says he's "angry at the people who thought up this plot to embarrass all of us they fired."
   a. What is the "plot to embarrass all of us they fired" to which he refers?
   b. Why is he angry at those people?

(5) The third paragraph says that Zarward acknowledged "violation of the company's written policy."
   a. Why, then, does he feel he should have had a warning before being fired?
   b. Why does he feel that firing was too severe a penalty?

(6) Why did Balenge think he could violate the company's policy and not get fired for it?

(7) Considering that Balenge knew about the company policy, what does he imply in his statement, "I wouldn't have done it if I'd known the company was going to fire me for it"? (Choose from the answers below.)
   a. I didn't think the policy was to be taken seriously.
   b. I didn't think I'd get fired for violating the policy.
   c. It's OK to violate a company's rules on purpose even though they're paying you to work for them.
   d. The company you work for should not fire you even if you violate one of their standards on purpose.

7. Someone suggested to Mr. Goldenstein that he do something he did not think was quite right to do. "It's OK, Abie," the person said. "Everyone does it." Mr. Goldenstein answered, "Don't tell me, 'Everybody does it.' What other people do is on their consciences, but what I do is on mine."

(1) Do you think Mr. Goldenstein is likely to go along with something because "everybody does it"? Explain.

(2) Do you think Mr. Goldenstein should go along with something because "everybody does it"? Explain.

8. What propaganda technique is being used when someone says, "Oh, come on. It's OK. Everybody does it"?

9. Should you believe someone who says to you, "Everybody does it"?

7.5 WHERE DO YOU DRAW THE LINE?

To say that doing something is acceptable is not the same as saying that doing it is perfectly honest.

Example:

Amy sees a penny lying on the sidewalk and sees no one around who might have dropped it. Amy picks up the penny and keeps it without trying to find the owner.

Most people would say that what Amy did was acceptable. But the perfectly honest thing to do would be to try to locate the person who lost the penny so that she could return it to him.

If you agree that keeping the penny is acceptable, then you have the problem of, "Where do you draw the line?" That is, suppose it were a $50 bill instead of a penny. Would it still be acceptable just to pick it up and keep it without trying to find the owner?

Notice that you are not being asked what you would really do. You are being asked what is acceptable for you to do. Somewhere along the way, an amount could be named which would cause you to say, "No, it's not acceptable for me just to pick it up and keep it without trying to find out who lost it." This means that there is a line somewhere between that amount and the amount which you said was acceptable to keep. On one side of the line, it is acceptable to keep what you found without trying to locate the owner. On the other side of the line, it is not acceptable to keep what you found without trying to locate the owner.

There are a great many situations in life where you must make a decision of where to draw a line. Once you draw a line, you then have to decide whether or not you will live your life according to where the line is drawn. It is one thing to be honestly mistaken about where a line is drawn, but it is a different thing to try to respect yourself if you know where a line is drawn and then you ignore it when you do something.

CLASS DISCUSSION PROBLEMS

Problems 1-16: In each case, a situation is described and is followed by one or more names with question marks after them. Tell whether or not you think the actions of the people in question were acceptable.

1. Grace eats at a restaurant and pays the cashier for her meal. There are some mints on the counter and Grace asks the cashier how much they are. The cashier answers, "They're a nickle each, but that's OK. Go ahead and take a couple." Grace takes two mints without paying for them. Cashier? Grace?

2. Ms. Kalloway is a carpenter for a construction company. The foreman tells the workers, "All this stuff in this pile is scrap as far as the company is concerned. It'll be hauled away in the next couple of days, so if any of you want to take some of it home, go ahead. It's free." Ms. Kalloway took home some lumber and fencing from the pile. Foreman? Ms. Kalloway?

3. Ms. Kalloway also needed some nails, so she took home some nails which were not in the pile the foreman had pointed out. Ms. Kalloway?

4. Linda is on a salary which allows her vacation time and an additional ten days a year for illness. She wakes up one morning and isn't ill but just doesn't feel like going to work. She calls in and tells them she's ill, and she takes the day off. Linda?

5. Ms. Uberman was going on a business trip. Her husband told her, "I'll be worried unless I know you got there safely. Call me when you get there. Place the call person-to-person and ask for yourself. I'll say you're not here, so I won't be lying, but I'll know you're OK and we won't have to pay for the call." Ms. Uberman did as her husband said. Mr. Uberman? Ms. Uberman?

6. Hedda got a candy bar from a vending machine by putting slugs into the machine. Hedda?

7. Todd heard that Nick was going around telling people that Todd was a liar and a coward, so Todd found Nick and punched him in the mouth. Todd?

8. Larry had been goofing off the past week and was now taking a test. He didn't know the answers, but he knew he could've learned the material if he'd studied. Miguel, one of the best students, sat beside him. Larry decided that it didn't make any difference whether he got the answers by studying or by copying from Miguel, so he copied Miguel's answers. Larry?

9. Miguel knew that Larry was copying from him and he didn't try to cover his paper so that Larry couldn't copy. Miguel?

10. Greg sat on the other side of Miguel, and Greg didn't know the answers, either. Greg had paid attention in class and had tried to learn the material but just couldn't understand it. He copied Miguel's answers. Greg?

11. Miguel knew that Greg was copying from him and he didn't try to cover his paper so that Greg couldn't copy. Miguel?

12. Sheila sat behind Miguel and was trying to see his answers. Miguel slouched down in his seat so that Sheila could see his paper better. Sheila? Miguel?

13. Amy sees a penny lying on the sidewalk and sees no one around who might have dropped it. Amy picks up the penny and keeps it without trying to find the owner. Amy?

14. Suppose it was a $1 bill instead of a penny which Amy found and kept without trying to find the owner. Amy?

15. Suppose it was money paper-clipped together totalling $500 which Amy found and kept without trying to find the owner. Amy?

16. Suppose that instead of finding the $1 bill on the sidewalk, Amy found it lying in the hall of an elementary school and that she kept it without trying to find the owner. Amy?

17. The following article appeared in Big City's newspaper.

Newmore quit W.B.C. in sadness, not as a public protest, he says

Jordan Newmore, in charge of the large public relations staff of World Wide Broadcasting Corporation until he resigned last week, said he quite his $45,000-a-year position because of "an irreconcilable difference in viewpoints" between him and Leonard Tolbar, president of W.B.C.

"I announced Mr. Tolbar's decision to broadcast certain programs during prime viewing time," Newmore said, "but I just couldn't see airing these programs at all, let alone during times the whole family is watching." Newmore said he and Tolbar have been friends for 22 years. He said they have had disagreements before over various decisions, "but these were differences of opinion with good and bad points on both sides of the issue. Although I often felt that his viewpoints were not the best, I could still justify them to the public."

Public outcries against Tolbar's decision were further heightened by the news of Newmore's resignation. "I'm not trying to lead a public protest on this," Newmore said in a lengthy interview. "It was a very personal decision. I wasn't angry with Mr. Tolbar."

"When I first heard of the decision, I had a sinking feeling and wondered how I could live with it," Newmore said. "I didn't see how I could try to justify this decision to the public. I have a bottom line on some things, and I knew that this was my bottom line. So I handed my resignation to Mr. Tolbar the next morning before making the announcement of his decision."

Newmore said there was no discussion of trying to change Tolbar's mind at that time, and he insisted that his letter of resignation was not an attempt to cause such a change. Newmore refuses to discuss details of the letter, saying that such details must come from Tolbar if they are to be made public.

Newmore said that he and Tolbar "shook hands and parted sorrowfully, at least on my part and, I hope, on his part, too."

(1) Why did Newmore resign his position with W.B.C.?

(2) According to Newmore's statements, we can infer that he tried to justify to the public some of Tolbar's previous

7.6 ATTRIBUTES OF A GOOD ARGUMENT

In order to decide whether or not an argument is a good one, we can start by agreeing that a good argument must have true premises, it must not use circular reasoning, and it must have a logical conclusion.

Example 1:

Most dogs are four-legged animals. All four-legged animals are cats. So most dogs are cats.

This is not a good argument. It is noncircular, and it has a logical conclusion, but the second premise is false.

Example 2:

Most dogs are four-legged animals. Most cats are four-legged animals. So most dogs are cats.

This is not a good argument. It has true premises and it is non-circular, but it does not have a logical conclusion.[1]

Example 3:

Most dogs are four-legged animals. Most cats are four-legged animals. So most dogs are four-legged animals.

This is not a good argument. The premises are true and the conclusion is logical, but the argument uses circular reasoning.

The trouble with everyday arguments is that the truth values of the premises are sometimes matters of opinion.

Example 4:

"Mrs. Overmore, your dog is vicious. Vicious dogs which are not kept under control should be impounded. So your dog should be impounded."

Here, the person is trying to convince Mrs. Overmore that her dog

---

[1]Notice that the conclusion in Example 2 is exactly the same as the conclusion in Example 1, and yet we're saying that the Example 2 conclusion is not logical, and the Example 1 conclusion is logical. This is because we judge a conclusion to be logical or not according to whether or not it has to follow from the premises. In Example 1, if we accept the premises as true, then the conclusion must be true.. But in Example 2, we can accept the premises as true and the conclusion still does not have to be true.

149

should be impounded. But if Mrs. Overmore does not agree that her dog is vicious, or if she thinks that her dog is kept under control, then she will not think that the argument is a good one.

Then we should also agree that if the truth value of a premise is a matter of opinion, a good argument should either tell what's wrong with the opposing opinion or it should support its own opinion.

Example 5:

"Mrs. Overmore, your dog snaps and barks fiercely at everyone who goes past your house. He tries to jump the fence and he keeps the neighborhood children terrorized. So your dog is vicious. Yesterday the gate was open and he got out and chased 5-year-old Marcia all the way home, so your dog is not kept under control. Vicious dogs which are not kept under control should be impounded. So your dog should be impounded."

At this point, Mrs. Overmore can do one of three things: she can disagree that the examples given show that her dog is vicious and is not kept under control; she can disagree with the sentence, "Vicious dogs which are not kept under control should be impounded"; or she can admit that the argument is a good one. If she does either of the first two things but does not give good reasons for her disagreement, then we will still say that the argument is a good one.

As you can tell from the previous sentence, an argument does not have to be airtight in order to be a good argument. But it should have strong support for any premise which is a matter of opinion. It was stated in section 7.3 that problem 6 of section 5.6 is an example of a good emotional argument. Let's take another look at that argument:

Example 6:

Big City's television shows are interrupted by a special bulletin: "Half an hour ago, a devastating tornado struck Midvale, just 20 miles from Big City. Scores of people were killed, and hundreds —maybe thousands—were injured. Many of the injured have suffered huge losses of blood, and it is estimated that the Red Cross emergency blood supply will be completely consumed within two hours. The Red Cross has issued an urgent request to the public for immediate donations of blood of all types."

The argument here is, "Hundreds or thousands of people need blood transfusions. There is not enough blood in the present emergency supply to meet these needs. So if you are able to donate blood, you should do so at once." Some of the premises are unstated but are taken for granted. For example, one such premise is, "Unless we obtain an additional supply of blood, many of these people will die." If you are the kind of person who does not want people to die if you can prevent their deaths, then the argument is a good one. If you are the kind of person who is indifferent about whether or not other people die when you could prevent their deaths, then the argument is not a good one.

Summary:
An argument is a good argument if and only if it
1. is noncircular and
2. has a logical conclusion and

150

3a. either has true premises, or
3b. has strong support for any premise which is a matter of opinion.

Notice that you do not have to like or agree with a conclusion in order to recognize that an argument is a good one.

CLASS DISCUSSION PROBLEMS

1. The crime rate in Big City was alarmingly high. The campaign slogan of a candidate for mayor of Big City was, "I'll make Big City as safe as Fort Knox!" When newspaper reporters asked the candidate for details on how he would accomplish this, he replied, "I'm not going to tell you how. Once I tell you how, the big-name candidates will steal my ideas, and then I won't have a chance of winning the election."

   (1) Does the candidate assume that he has a chance of winning the election if he doesn't tell the reporters the details of his plan? Explain.
   (2) What do you think of the candidate's reason for not telling the details of his plan? Explain.
   (3) Is the candidate's argument a good one? Explain.

2. A candidate for governor of Midstate said, "A good governor of Midstate must have the six most important characteristics needed for his office: a love of Midstate, reliability, willingness to work, honesty, a sense of responsibility, and ability. I have all of these characteristics, so a vote for me will be a vote for a good governor."

   What's wrong with his argument?

3. A weekly advertising paper mailed to residents of three counties of Midstate has the following printed in the upper right corner of the first page:

   > "JUNK" MAIL?
   > This publication paid
   > $126,749.53
   > postage last year!

   (1) What appears to be the purpose of printing these words? The purpose appears to be (choose one)
      a. to tell how much postage they paid last year.
      b. to imply that the paper has a wide circulation.
      c. to convince the reader that this paper is not "junk" mail.
      d. to let the reader know that the paper was also published last year.
   (2) Restate the boxed words in the form of an argument, including a premise which is not stated but is taken for granted.
   (3) Is the argument a good one? Explain.

4. Ms. Poruka teaches physics. She knows her subject well, spends time preparing for each lesson, and often gives her students extra study guides to help them understand ideas.

She presents her lessons in an organized, understandable way, giving several examples to make sure the students can understand. However, some of her students talk noisily among themselves and so prevent other students from hearing her explanations. When someone mentions to Ms. Poruka that some of her students can't hear her, she replies, "It's my job to teach them, and it's their job to learn. I'm doing my job—I'm presenting the material to them so they can understand it if they want to. If they don't want to do their jobs, then that's <u>their</u> business, not mine. I'm doing my job whether or not they listen, so if they want to learn, all they have to do is keep quiet while I'm teaching."

(1) Do you agree with Ms. Poruka? Why?

(2) Ms. Poruka gives an argument for allowing students to talk during a lesson. Is her argument a good one? Explain.

(3) Consider the students who are not talking and cannot concentrate on the lesson because of the noise of other students. Assuming that Ms. Poruka is not going to change her ways and that they cannot transfer to another class, what can these students do to make the situation better for themselves?

(4) If you were a student in Ms. Poruka's class, what would you do
   a. if you really wanted to learn the material but were having a hard time because of all the noise around you?
   b. if you didn't care one way or another about learning the material?

5. Mark Twain said, "Truth is our most precious possession. Let us, therefore, be as economical as possible in our use of it." If we supply a missing premise, we can rewrite Twain's argument as follows: "Truth is our most precious possession. We should be economical in our use of any precious possession. So we should be as economical as possible in our use of truth."

Is this argument a good one? Why?

6. In speaking of Hitler's purges, Pastor Martin Niemoller said,

In Germany they first came for the Communists, and I didn't speak up because I wasn't a Communist. Then they came for the Jews, and I didn't speak up because I wasn't a Jew. Then they came for the trade unionists, and I didn't speak up because I wasn't a trade unionist. Then they came for the Catholics, and I didn't speak up because I was a Protestant. Then they came for me— and by that time no one was left to speak up.

Is this a good argument for protesting unfair treatment of someone even though you are not being treated unfairly yourself? Why?

7. Go back to example 3 in section 5.3.
   a. Of what is Roy trying to convince the listener?
   b. Is Roy's argument good, so-so, or poor? Explain.

8. Go back to problem 2 in section 5.4. You will notice that most of the speaker's comments are directed against his opponent.
   a. Of what is the speaker trying to convince us?
   b. Is his argument good, so-so, or poor? Explain.

7.7 CLASS DISCUSSION PROBLEMS AND QUESTIONS FOR CHAPTER REVIEW

1. Gloria works as a waitress for a big restaurant chain. Two or three times a week, Gloria takes home some odds and ends from the restaurant—perhaps some sugar cubes, or some book matches, or some napkins, or half a loaf of bread, or part of a roll of paper towels. Is this acceptable?
2. Cindy works as a cashier at the end of a self-service line for the same restaurant chain. Each Friday, Cindy rings up on the register about $1 less than she collects, and she keeps the difference. Is this acceptable?
3. Restate each sentence so that only neutral words and phrases are used and so that the same meaning is kept.
   a. "That's a bunch of rot!"
   b. "He's a wet blanket."
   c. "The prices they charge are highway robbery!"
4. Each of the following is a rule in our society. Tell why we have this rule.
   a. Say, "Thank you," when someone does a favor for you.
   b. Cover your mouth when you cough or sneeze.
   c. Don't talk with food in your mouth.
   d. Don't tell harmful lies about someone.
5. a. Why do we have to pay taxes?
   b. When filing a state or federal income tax return, is it acceptable to fudge a little on reporting income or deductions? Explain.
6. Go back to problem 3 in section 5.6. This is an argument for having remodeling done now instead of waiting until later. Is this argument good, so-so, or poor? Explain.
7. In section 5.10, problem 1 is an argument to vote for the speaker. Is this argument good, so-so, or poor? Explain.
8. Look again at problem 2 in section 5.10.
   a. Of what is the speaker trying to convince us?
   b. Is his argument good, so-so, or poor? Explain.
9. Look again at problem 4 in section 5.10.
   a. Of what is the speaker trying to convince us?
   b. Is the argument good, so-so, or poor? Explain.
10. Example 1 in section 5.11 is an argument.
    a. Of what does the argument try to convince us?
    b. Is the argument good, so-so, or poor? Explain.
11. Read problem 5 in section 5.11 again.
    a. Of what is the speaker trying to convince us?
    b. Is his argument good, so-so, or poor? Explain.

12. In section 5.12, problem 8 proposes a way to get drunk drivers off the road.
    a.   What is this solution?
    b.   Do you think this solution is good, so-so, or poor? Explain.
13. Where is the line between "everyone should be allowed to do his own thing" and "you should stop doing your own thing and work together with others for the common good"? (Or is there such a line?)
14. Where is the line between "live and let live" and showing some opposition to what's going on?
15. Where is the line between "sticking your nose into someone else's business" and "doing your duty as a responsible citizen"?
16. What's the difference between tattling and doing your duty as a citizen? (When does informing stop being undesirable and start being a duty?)
17. What's wrong with having double standards?

CHAPTER 8

LEARNING TO BE
OPEN-MINDED

8.1   INTRODUCTION

8.2   LOOKING AT TWO SIDES OF AN ISSUE

8.3   RECOGNIZING ISSUES AND SUPPORTING POINTS

8.4   ANTICIPATING ARGUMENTS FOR THE OTHER SIDE

8.5   FINDING ARGUMENTS OF YOUR OWN

8.6   DEBATING

8.7   CLASS DISCUSSION PROBLEMS AND QUESTIONS
        FOR CHAPTER REVIEW

8.1 INTRODUCTION

One of the hardest things to do in thinking is to learn to look at a question from more than one side, especially if we already have an opinion about the answer.

Poor thinking usually goes something like this:

1. We recognize what is being asked.
2. We get an answer for the time being.
3. We think of reasons to support our answer.
4. We are vague about why a different answer is wrong.
5. We feel pretty sure that because our answer is right, another answer can't have much to support it.
6. If weak spots are found in our reasons for our answer, we try to defend them instead of thinking about them.
7. When someone tries to tell us why his answer is better, we ignore his reasons.
8. When all else fails, we get upset at being questioned about it.

But good thinking usually goes something like this:

1. We recognize what is being asked.
2. We try to think of as many possible answers as we can.
3. We try to think of reasoning to support each answer.
4. We discard answers which are supported only by weak reasoning.
5. We choose the answer supported by the best reasoning.
6. When someone questions our choice, we give the reasons for our choice and also tell what we think is wrong with the other choices.
7. If the person points out a weakness in our own reasoning, we think about it carefully before deciding whether or not he is right.
8. If someone brings up a new reason for a different choice, we think about it carefully before deciding whether or not to change our minds.

The purpose of this chapter is to teach you not only how to support your own opinion but how to anticipate what the other person is likely to say. In other words, you should learn to look honestly at more than one side of a question.

CLASS DISCUSSION PROBLEMS

1. See item 5 on the "poor thinking" list in this section. What's wrong with feeling this way?
2. See item 6 on the "poor thinking" list. What's wrong with doing this?
3. What's wrong with items 2 and 3 on the "poor thinking" list?
4. What's wrong with item 4 on the "poor thinking" list?
5. Have you ever known someone to get angry about having an opinion or judgment questioned, even though the questions were not meant to arouse anger? If so, describe at least one such incident.

8.2 LOOKING AT TWO SIDES OF AN ISSUE

As the first step toward learning to look at more than one side of a question, each of the problems which follows lists a question which has two possible answers and then lists good reasons for choosing each answer.

When you are deciding which side to take, remember that this section is intended to help you learn to think critically. Choose the side for which you can argue better, even though you may not personally agree with that side.

Save all of your homework from this section. You'll need it later.

CLASS DISCUSSION PROBLEMS

For each problem, do three things:
(a) Tell which side you agree with.
(b) Find something wrong with each argument given for the <u>other</u> side.
(c) Give at least one argument of <u>your own</u> for your side.

1. Should Student Council members be elected by teachers instead of by students?
   Those who say "yes" give these reasons:
   (1) Teachers often see leadership qualities in a student which the students themselves do not see. Election of SC members by the teachers would make use of these leadership qualities.
   (2) Teachers know the grades of their students, whereas the students themselves often have only vague knowledge about the grades of fellow students. Using these grades, teachers would be more likely than students to elect SC members who can afford to devote the time necessary to having a successful SC.
   (3) It also follows from (2) above that the intellectual level of SC members would be higher if SC members were chosen by the teachers than if they were chosen by the students.
   Those who say "no" give these reasons:
   (1) The SC should be a <u>student</u> council. If members are elected by the teachers instead of by the students, the students are likely to feel that the SC is not theirs but belongs to the teachers.
   (2) A teacher does not know a student as well as other students know him. It is unlikely that a teacher-chosen SC member would represent the majority of students.
   (3) If teachers were to elect SC members, the students so elected would be singled out as "teacher's pets" and would be embarrassed by this, whereas if they were elected by the students, they would be honored rather than embarrassed.

2. Should part of a course grade be based on attendance? (For this question, we will assume that the course is not one where the participation of each student is necessary to the success of the class—such as in choir, band, or team sports, for example.)

   Those who say "yes" give these reasons:
   (1) A student who has been absent doesn't know what's going on at first, and he holds up the progress of the class by asking about things which were taught while he was absent. He should be penalized for this.
   (2) If a student knows that part of his grade is based on attendance, he's more likely not to skip and so he'll learn more.

   Those who say "no" give these reasons:
   (1) A student should be graded on how much he knows about a subject and not on whether or not he was in class when he learned it.
   (2) If you start grading on attendance, you have to think about the student who misses a lot of classes because of sickness. Either he'll get a lower grade because he missed so many classes, or you'll make an exception for sickness. If he gets a lower grade, he's being penalized for something which wasn't his fault. If you make an exception for illness, then you're using a double standard, because you're saying to one student, "You missed a lot of classes, but your grade won't be lower," and at the same time you're saying to another student, "You missed the same number of classes as the other kid, and your grade will be lower."

3. Should final examinations be required in high school subjects?

   Arguments for the "yes" side:
   (1) A teacher doesn't really know how much of the material his students have learned until he gives a test on it. Both right answers and wrong answers to final exam questions can give the teacher information about the effectiveness of his teaching methods.
   (2) Workers often need to know how to organize and summarize their knowledge. For example, the typist, the machine operator, and the engineer all may be asked to break in a new worker and teach him how to do the work. Studying for and writing the answers to a final exam help the student learn to summarize and organize his knowledge.

   Arguments for the "no" side:
   (1) Everyone has a bad day once in a while—a headache, a fight with a "steady," home problems, temporary inability to concentrate. If a final exam day is one of those bad days, the student's grade for a whole semester of conscientious work could be lowered by as much as a whole grade or more.
   (2) Final exams are sometimes just thrown together without much thought for content or importance of material. As

an indication of the material learned in a course, such exams do not give worthwhile information either to the student or to the teacher.

4. Should high school students who take a course be grouped by ability, or not?

   Arguments for the "yes" side:

   (1) It isn't fair to the slow student to schedule him into the same class as a fast student. Too often a fast student will see and comment on some far-reaching generalization of something taught and the slow student will get discouraged, thinking he's supposed to understand everything that's going on. As a result, he stops trying and so doesn't learn.

   (2) If we put students of all abilities in the same class, the teacher can't teach all of them at the same time. So where does he aim his teaching? If to the fast student, then the averge student struggles to keep up and the slow student is lost. If to the average student, then the slow student struggles to keep up and the fast student is bored. If to the slow student, then both average and fast students are bored. No matter where he aims his teaching, the teacher is likely to have discipline problems, and the students are not learning as much as they could learn in a class containing only students of similar abilities.

   Arguments for the "no" side:

   (1) Too many high school students are just plain lazy. They give their counselors and their teachers the "dumb" act in order to get scheduled into a slower group just so they won't have to put in an honest effort to pass the class. We're certainly not doing such students any favors when we don't at least expect them to use their abilities.

   (2) Research has shown that many teachers tend to teach according to what they believe their students' abilities to be. [That is a true statement.] As a result, the teacher of a slow group is likely to believe that these students are not capable of learning much and he will teach accordingly. It's hard to believe that such a student will learn more this way than if grouped with the averge and fast students where at least he is given the chance to learn more.

5. Should a student's grade be based on effort as well as achievement?

   Teachers who answer "yes" give these reasons:

   (1) What do we teach a student by flunking him when he's tried his best? We teach him that effort doesn't count for anything, and that is certainly not true in the outside world. In many jobs, effort and reliability are more important than brains.

   (2) We're always complaining because we get kids who don't want to do any work. If the kids knew they'd pass

just for _trying_ to do the work, maybe we'd have more kids who'd try to learn.

(3) It isn't fair to the student to flunk him when he's tried to learn the material. Who knows? If he'd had a different teacher, maybe the tests would've been easier and he'd have passed without any added credit for effort. Why penalize the student for not having a teacher who gives easier tests?

Teachers who answer "no" give these reasons:

(1) If you want to raise a student's grade for good effort, then to be consistent you'd have to lower a student's grade for poor effort. This isn't fair to the student who was put into the class against his wishes but who decides to make the best of it and does just enough work to get by.

(2) How can you _really_ tell which students are trying to do the work and which ones aren't trying? A student can sound very sincere when he's telling you he tried but just _couldn't_ do the homework when he actually just goofed off watching TV the night before.

(3) A grade is supposed to reflect knowledge of subject matter. Suppose you have three students—Carol, Doris, and Janet. Carol tries hard but doesn't know the first thing about what's going on. Doris is bright and doesn't hardly try at all, but she has a C average. Janet is a little slow, her effort is about average, and she has a D average. If you're going to count effort in the grades, all three students will end up with D's, but their knowledge of the subject is most certainly not the same.

8.3 RECOGNIZING ISSUES AND SUPPORTING POINTS

In the preceding set of problems, arguments for each side of a question were numbered so that you could tell what they were. But in everyday life, we do not often find positions and arguments so neatly labelled. In everyday life, the speaker may or may not state his position right away. He may or may not say, "first," "second," and so on, to help us follow his thinking.

Even when he does, it is sometimes hard to tell the difference between the main point he is trying to make (the conclusion of his argument) and the reasons he gives to support this main point (the premises of his argument).

Example:

In problem 5 of the section 8.2 problems, the "no" side gives three arguments. This means the "no" side made three main points. These points are: (1) it is unfair to lower the grade of a student who didn't want the class but decides to do just enough work to get by; (2) the teacher can't be sure of how much effort a student is putting into the class; (3) a grade which includes

160

effort will not show knowledge of the subject. The other statements for the "no" side are reasons to support these main points.

The next set of problems should help you learn to recognize (1) what question is being argued, (2) what side the speaker is taking, (3) what main points the speaker is making, and (4) what opposing arguments the speaker anticipates and refutes.

Save all of your homework papers from this section for later use.

CLASS DISCUSSION PROBLEMS

For each problem, someone's viewpoint is stated and supported. As you read, look for the question being argued, the side being taken, the main points being made, and whether or not the writer anticipates and refutes arguments for the opposing viewpoint. Answer the questions which follow each argument.

1. We should have a law stating that parents should be held financially responsible for the acts of their kids until the kids reach the age of 18. Without such a law, a kid can damage someone's property and the victim has to pay for it himself unless the parents volunteer to pay for it. But not all parents will offer to pay for the damage, and it is unfair for the victim to have to pay for it himself.

    If you think that such a law would be unfair to the parents, since parents cannot always control their kids, consider this: if we had such a law, parents would be more careful about teaching their kids to respect the property of others. And they'd pay more attention to where their kids go and what they're supposed to be doing there. If a parent still can't control his kid, let him turn the kid over to the law.

    (1) What is the question being argued? (Choose one.)
    a. Is it unfair to expect a victim of theft or property damage to pay for the damage himself?
    b. Should parents do a better job of raising and controlling their children?
    c. Should we have a law stating that parents will be held financially responsible for their child's acts until the child is 18?
    d. Should parents volunteer to pay for property damage caused by their child?

    (2) Which side does the writer take?
    (3) The writer lists one main point to support his side. Briefly, what is this main point?
    (4) The writer anticipates and refutes an argument for the opposite side.
    a. What is this argument?
    b. How does the writer refute this argument?

    (5) Do you think the writer's idea is a good one, or not? Explain.

161

2.   No makeup tests should be given unless a student misses two or more tests in a row because of a single extended illness. If a teacher allows makeup tests, either he gives the same test or he prepares a different test for the student who was absent. If he gives the same test, then it is unfair to the students who took the test on time, since the absent student not only had a longer time to study for the test but also had the chance to find out what was on it. If the teacher prepares a different test, then it is unfair to the teacher, since he then must spend his personal time for the benefit of the student who was absent.

    Too many students simply skip school when they are not prepared for a test, knowing that they will be allowed to take a makeup test. If makeup tests were eliminated, such students would learn better study habits, for they would know that they either had to take the test or get a zero for missing it. When a teacher gives makeup tests, there will be at least one student absent for nearly every test; but when a teacher does not give makeup tests, every student is there for nearly every test. This shows that it is not usually illness which causes students to be absent on test days.

    To prevent unjust treatment of the student who is really absent because of illness, the teacher can drop the lowest test grade for every student. Thus, every student can miss one test and not be penalized in his grade. To prevent unfairness to students who have made previous commitments for a test date—such as medical appointments or out-of-town trips with parents—test dates can be announced in advance in order to make sure that the dates are clear for all students.

    (1) What is the question being argued?
    (2) What is the writer's position on the question?
    (3) The writer makes two main points for his position. What are these main points?
    (4) The writer anticipates and refutes two arguments of the opposing side.
       (a) What are these arguments?
       (b) How does the writer refute each of these arguments?
    (5) Do you agree with the writer's viewpont, or not? Explain.

3.   A student should be allowed to get credit for a high school course by taking a special examination. I'm talking about the ordinary course, not the course where group effort is necessary, such as choir or drama. Some students are bright enough to sit down with a textbook and read it by themselves and understand it. To require such a student to sign up for the course, do the homework, take every little quiz and test given, and do whatever else is usually required for a good grade is a waste of his time. He could spend this time better in some course for which he needs a teacher's instruction. Furthermore, to put him in a course for which he doesn't need a teacher's instruction may be a waste of the taxpayers' money, for if the course is filled, he is probably preventing some other student from taking it.

To say that you can't fairly base a grade for a whole course on one exam is ridiculous. In the first place, colleges regularly offer credit by special examination. In the second place, you're probably thinking of a normal one-hour exam, but I'm talking about a special exam—it can last five or six hours, if you like. And don't give me that old excuse that some things taught in a course can't be measured by an examination. If these things can't be measured by an exam, then you don't know whether or not the students in the regular course are learning these things, either, so this is not a logical reason for not allowing credit by special exam.

(1) What is the question being argued?
(2) What side does the writer take?
(3) The writer makes two main points to support his side. What are these points?
(4) The writer anticipates and refutes two arguments for the opposing side.
  (a) What are these arguments?
  (b) How does the writer refute each of these arguments?
(5) Do you agree with the writer's viewpoint, or not? Explain.

4. Let's start using common sense in our schools. We send our kids to school to learn how to read, write, spell, use the English language, and do arithmetic. But regardless of whether or not they're learning these things, their teachers throw in singing, art, gym, band, show-and-tell, assemblies, special projects, and all the other nonessential frills.

No wonder our kids get past the sixth grade without knowing how to read or spell or divide or put a sentence together properly! Kids tend to learn what they're expected to learn. The fact that all the frills are thrown in whether or not the basics are learned shows them that they're not really expected to learn the basics well, and so they don't learn them well.

It's time to start setting definite levels of achievement to be reached in each grade for reading, writing, spelling, grammar, and arithmetic. We should say that when and only when a kid reaches the required level on all of these, then he moves to the next grade. In the meantime, no art, no assemblies, no gym—no frills, period.

You may say, "What about science? What about geography?" We don't need separate times set aside for these. Get rid of the reading books with all the fairy tales and fiction, and get books which include science and geography. The kids will learn these things as part of their reading lessons. "But the kids enjoy reading fiction," you say. Sure they do. They can still check books out of the school library to read on their own time. But I'm saying I want my kids to learn the basics on school time. I don't want to pay for teaching kids about frills when they haven't yet learned the basics.

Don't tell me I don't realize the importance of art or singing or whatever in educating our children. I'm not against including such things at the junior and senior high levels—after the kids have learned the basics. Kids should spend the first half of their school years—grades 1-6—learning the basics and then spend the next half—grades 7-12—expanding on these basics and getting a broader education, including art, band, choir, a knowledge of literature, and whatever else you want to throw in.

(1) What is the question being argued by the writer? (Choose one.)
   a. Are we using common sense in our schools?
   b. Should the teaching of science and geography be eliminated in our elementary schools?
   c. Should such things as art, singing, and gym be eliminated in our schools?
   d. Should our elementary schools eliminate everything except reading, writing, spelling, grammar, and arithmetic?

(2) What position does the writer take on this question?

(3) The writer gives two main points to support his position. What are they?

(4) The writer anticipates and refutes three arguments of the opposing side.
   (a) What are these arguments?
   (b) How does the writer refute each of these arguments?

(5) Do you think that if the writer's suggestion were adopted, sixth-grade graduates would know the basics better than they do using our present methods? Explain.

(6) Do you favor the writer's suggestion? Explain.

8.4 ANTICIPATING ARGUMENTS FOR THE OTHER SIDE

In each of the problems in section 8.3, the writer not only had arguments for his own side but he also anticipated what his opponents might say. In everyday life we are often in situations where we should anticipate what the arguments are for an opposing viewpoint, and we should have good answers ready to refute them.

For example, suppose you want to ask your boss for a raise. It would be kind of silly just to walk in thinking that he won't have any good reasons for not wanting to give you a raise, and if you don't have good refutations ready, you probably won't get the raise.

Or suppose you think a teacher has been unfair in grading you and you go to see him about it. You'd better realize first that hardly any teacher grades unfairly on purpose, so he must think he has a good reason for giving you that grade. It follows that you'd better try to figure out what those reasons might be <u>before</u> you see the teacher so that you can have refutations ready.

CLASS DISCUSSION PROBLEMS

Problems 1-4: Answer each question with as many <u>good</u> reasons as you can think of.

1. You've worked at the same place for five years and the only pay raise you've had is a raise six months after you started. You think you deserve more money and you decide to ask the boss for another raise. Assuming that he can afford to give you the raise, why might he not want to do so?

2. You are a 17-year-old girl who lives in a nice neighborhood where there have been no violent crimes for the past four years. A local department store, only five blocks away, is advertising for a salesgirl to work from 6-10 p.m. three nights a week. Why might your parents object to your taking the job?

3. Many of your friends smoke marijuana and have urged you to try it. They've told you of some of its effects and make it sound exciting.

    (a) You've told them that you don't care to try it but still they keep after you to try it. Why might they be so persistent about getting you to try it?

    (b) You know your parents are dead set against it even though they've never tried it themselves. Why might they be so much against it when they don't even know what it's like?

4. Suppose you apply for a job in which you'll have some contact with the employer's customers—say as a receptionist, or a salesperson, or a stock or delivery person—and you wear faded jeans and a frayed sweatshirt to the interview and use poor grammar in answering questions you are asked. Also suppose that you are bright, energetic, and very willing to work for the money you'll be paid. Also suppose that you see someone else waiting to apply for the same job and that this other person uses proper grammar and is dressed in clothes more suited to applying for a job. If this other person would be only fair at the job and you'd be very good at it, and if the employer knows this, then why might he still decide to hire the other person instead of you?

5. Students often ask teachers for letters of recommendation—perhaps for a job, or a club membership, or a scholarship, or acceptance at a college. Ms. Rabowitz feels that the student is trying to better himself in such a case, and she says, "I always give a good recommendation. Who am I to try to judge this student and say he'll be a flop at what he wants to do? Getting accepted may be just what he needs, and he may surprise all of us by getting on the ball and being very successful." Ms. Chou, too, feels that the student is trying to better himself, but she says, "Recommendations are supposed to mean something, and this student has chosen me to judge him to the best of my ability and knowledge of him. There are many students who've worked up to their abilities and honestly deserve the things they're trying for, and there are others who've just been goofing off and getting by, and I think it's dishonest to write anything other than my true opinion in such a letter."

(1) What is the question on which Ms. Rabowitz and Ms. Chou disagree? (Choose one.)
   a. Should a teacher be truthful about recommendations given for a student?
   b. Should a student ask a teacher for a recommendation?
   c. If a student asks a teacher for a recommendation, should the teacher give him one?
   d. If a student asks a teacher for a recommendation, is the student trying to better himself?
(2) Which side does
   (a) Ms. Rabowitz take?
   (b) Ms. Chou take?
(3) With which side do you agree?
(4) List all of the main points given for the <u>other</u> side.
(5) List at least one additional argument for the <u>other</u> side.

8.5 FINDING ARGUMENTS OF YOUR OWN

By this time, you should be fairly good at recognizing both the question being argued and the main points being given to support a viewpoint. The next set of problems will give you practice in finding good arguments for opposing sides of a question.

Save all of your homework papers from this section for later use.

CLASS DISCUSSION PROBLEMS

Problems 1-6: Give <u>at least</u> one <u>good</u> argument for <u>each</u> side of the question.

1. Should fairy tales be included in the books used in reading classes for elementary school children?
2. Should supermarkets stay open 24 hours a day?
3. Should every child aged five or over be given regular home chores to do, these chores to be within his capabilities?
4. Should every child aged seven or over be given a set weekly allowance to spend as he pleases?
5. Should students be allowed to chew gum in school?
6. Should true-false tests be given in school?

Problems 7-12: Give at least <u>two</u> <u>good</u> arguments for <u>each</u> side of the question.

7. Should multiple-choice tests be given in school?
8. Should junior high and senior high school students attend classes six days a week?
9. Should career information be included at all of grade levels K-14?
10. Assuming that he satisfies any requirements his state has for graduation, should a high school student be allowed to take any classes he wants to take and then graduate when he accumulates a certain number of credits?
11. Should high school students be required to learn some materials from their textbooks with no explanations from their teachers, assuming these materials are carefully chosen by their teachers?
12. Should students in American high schools be taught what communism is?

8.6 DEBATING

So far, the problems in this book have all been designed to give you time to think about what you want to say. You've had some practice in thinking fast when you've taken part in and listened to the class discussions. In the class discussions, however, you probably seldom had the burden of arguing completely without hope of support from your classmates.

By this time, you're supposed to have learned how to recognize an opponent's main points (section 8.3), how to refute them (section 8.2), and how to anticipate them (sections 8.4 and 8.5).

Now we'll see how well you can do at combining all of these, along with thinking of good arguments for your own viewpoint. And just to make it tougher, you'll have to give your arguments and your refutations while standing in front of the class.

Here's the way it'll work:

1. You and a classmate choose a debatable question[1] to argue about in front of the class. (You don't have to choose from the questions in this textbook.)
2. Decide together which terms need to be defined and how they are to be defined so that you are both arguing about the same question.

---

[1] A debatable question must have two characteristics: first, it must be able to be answered "yes" or "no"; second, it must have reasonably good points which can be made for both sides. All of the problems in section 8.5 and in this section are debatable questions. A question such as, "Which is prettier—blue, or green?" is not a debatable question, for it cannot be answered "yes" or "no." A question such as, "Is an elm tree a plant?" is not a debatable question, because it has no reasonably good arguments for the "no" side. A question such as, "Do you think . . . [so-and-so]?" is not a debatable question, for if I take the "yes" side, then the "no" side has no reasonably good arguments to tell me that I <u>don't</u> think the answer is "yes."

3. Agree on the date the question is to be argued in front of the class.
4. Each debater has two turns to argue. You get three minutes for your first turn and two minutes for your second turn. There is a one-minute rest period between turns (if the next debater wants it).
5. The "yes" debater starts. He must define the terms needing definition and must also present all of his main points during his first turn. If he does not define a term which his opponent asked to have defined (from item 2 above), then the "no" debater can define the term in any reasonable way he chooses.
6. The "no" debater gives all the main points for his side. It is courteous (but not <u>required</u>) for him to refute as many of the "yes" arguments as his time allows, thus giving the "yes" debater the chance to rebuild his arguments.
7. The "yes" debater refutes as many of his opponent's arguments as he can. He is also allowed to rebuild or support his own main points during this time, but he is not allowed to introduce new main points during this time.
8. The "no" debater refutes as many of his opponent's arguments as he can. He, too, is allowed to rebuild or support his own main points but is not allowed to introduce new main points during this time.
9. During a debater's turn, no one is allowed to talk except the debater himself. Between turns, other students may talk among themselves, but they must talk so that neither debater can overhear them.

A good way to upset your opponent so that he can't think straight when his turn comes is to <u>anticipate</u> what he's likely to say and refute it before he gets the chance to say it. (You say something like, "My opponent may say [so-and-so], but that's a weak argument because [such-and-such].") Then that part of his prepared debate has been neatly murdered. While he's trying to think of what to do about it, he isn't hearing what you're saying, so you're running your arguments right past him, and so it's unlikely that he'll refute them all.

Although neither debater is allowed to change the question once they have agreed on it, the "yes" debater may introduce a plan to make his answer practical.

Example 1:
Suppose the question is, "Should there be a law saying that a person is legally dead when his brain is no longer functioning?" The "yes" debater can say, "Yes. And in order to make sure that the law does what it is intended to do, it must also define the expression 'brain is no longer functioning.'"

Also, for some kinds of questions, the "no" debater may be able to destroy his opponent's argument almost completely by arguing for an alternate plan.

Example 2:
Suppose the question is, "Should career information be included at all of grade levels K-14?" The "no" debater can say, "No. It should be included only in all of grade levels 1-14. It

should not be included in kindergarten because [so-and-so]." He can then spend all the rest of his time giving reasons why it should not be included in kindergarten, at the same time anticipating and refuting his opponent's refutations of his argument. His opponent may have been expecting the "no" debater to argue that continuous career education through all the grade levels is unnecessary, and so he may be completely unprepared for the argument actually given.

CLASS DISCUSSION PROBLEMS

As discussed in this section, each question below is a debatable question. Choose one of these or one of your own to debate with a classmate. (If you can't find a classmate willing to debate against you on the question, see if you can talk your teacher into it.)

1. Should high school students be allowed to leave school during their study hall periods?
2. Should students who are not prohibited by state law from smoking in school be allowed to smoke ordinary cigarettes in school during the school day?
3. Should euthanasia (mercy killing) be allowed?
4. If a juvenile has been convicted of two separate felonies, should he be confined in a public institution?
5. Should anyone of age fifteen or over who is accused of committing or threatening to commit bodily harm with a lethal weapon be tried as an adult? (For the purpose of this question, assume that the accused person was the one who started the trouble.)
6. In a high school, should a student newspaper be entirely free to publish anything its student staff wants to publish?
7. Should the federal government have a law guaranteeing each family a minimum annual income?
8. Should there be capital punishment for persons convicted of such crimes as . . . .? (Get together with a classmate and decide what kinds of crimes you want to include.)
9. Should a high school student who is planning to go to college be required to take at least one year of a foreign language in high school?
10. Should a high school student who is not planning to go to college be required to take at least a year's worth of four- to six-week minicourses in various kinds of vocational training such as drafting, typing, machine shop, arts and crafts, book-keeping, wood shop, computer programming, auto repair?

8.7 CLASS DISCUSSION PROBLEMS AND QUESTIONS FOR CHAPTER REVIEW

1.   There is a wide difference of opinions among students as to how many and what kinds of tests should be given in a course. Among the opinions are these: some students say that a lot of minor tests and no major tests should be given; some say that no minor tests and only a few major tests should be given; some say that no tests at all should be given.

Students who favor a lot of minor tests and no major tests give these arguments:

(a) When you have a major test, too much of the grade depends on how you do on that one day. If you're not feeling well, your test results won't show what you know, and your grade will be lowered even though you know the material.

(b) Having a lot of minor tests keeps you from falling behind in learning the material, since you always feel there's another test coming up right away. Even if you put off studying until the last minute, you have only a few days' worth of material to learn instead of several weeks' worth.

Students who favor no minor tests and only a few major tests give these reasons:

(a) We already have too little time to learn what we're supposed to learn in each course, and every time we have a minor test, we're spending time taking a test which could be spent more profitably learning new material. Both the students and the teacher can find out what the students learned by having just a few major tests.

(b) Some students don't learn new material right away. They have to think it over a while. Throwing in minor tests keeps these students edgy, because they're always afraid they won't learn the material in time for the test and then their grades will suffer.

Students who favor no tests at all give these arguments:

(a) Regardless of whether or not tests are given, students who want to learn will learn, and students who don't want to learn won't learn. They may all pass the tests given, but the students who don't want to learn crammed for the test the night before and then forgot the material again by the following night. So test scores are not a reliable indication of the amount of lasting knowledge a student acquired.

(b) A teacher doesn't have to give tests to tell what a student has learned. He can tell from such things as homework, class participation, effort, and extra projects done.

(1) List the main points made by each side.
(2) Refute each of the six main points.
(3) State as many additional arguments as you can think of for <u>each</u> side.
(4) Refute as many of your own arguments as you can.

2. When you did the problems in section 8.2, you chose a side and then argued from that viewpoint. Go back to those problems now and redo them, choosing the other side of each problem this time.

3. When you did the problems in section 8.3, you were asked to list the writer's main points, but you were not asked to refute them. Go back to those problems now and see how many main points you can refute in each problem.

4 For the problems in section 8.5, you were asked to list one or two arguments for <u>each</u> side of each question. Go back now to those arguments you listed and see how many of them you can refute.

5. The following editorial appeared in a Big City newspaper:

For many years now, we have been able to keep a man's heart pumping, his blood flowing, his kidneys functioning—even though his brain is dead—and we have done these things because his kidneys or other organs could be used for transplants to give life, health, or sight to others.

Thus the modern miracles of medicine and engineering have combined to give us a critical legal problem: when is a person to be considered legally dead? Is it when we unplug the machine which keeps his heart beating? Is it when his brain-wave pattern is simply a straight line?

"What's the difference?" you might ask. The answer lies in the case of Edward Morburl, victim of a vicious beating on a Big City street last week.

Edward, 17 years old, was brought to Big City Emergency Hospital at 10:00 p.m. last Tuesday. Despite blood transfusions and surgery, his brain stopped functioning at 11:00 a.m. last Wednesday. His kidneys were healthy and his blood matched the type needed for kidney transplants for two little girls about to die. So the doctors hooked him up to a machine which kept his heart beating mechanically, hoping that his family might be willing to donate his kidneys to save the little girls.

Edward's mother, Mrs. Morburl, was ready to give her consent. But then the Big City medical examiner told her that when Edward's attackers are brought to trial for murder, the defense attorneys will be able to raise the question of whether "death" was caused by the beating or whether "death" was caused by removal of the kidneys.

With tears in her eyes and heart, Mrs. Morburl decided that the lives of the two little girls were more important than the conviction of her son's killers, and she gave her consent for the kidney transplants.

It will be bad enough if Edward's killers go free because a jury decides his death was caused by removal of his kidneys, but it will be even worse if such a situation is allowed to arise again. Here we have not only the problem of allowing murderers to go free but the possibility of bringing to trial for murder the operating team who removed the kidneys.

Our legislators could solve both problems by passing a law stating that a person can be considered legally dead when his brain stops functioning, regardless of whether or not mechanical devices are used to maintain his other signs of life.

(1) Of what is the writer trying to convince us?

(2) The writer makes two main points to support his side. What are they?

(3) Is the writer's argument emotional, or uemotional? Explain.

(4) Do you think the writer's argument is good, so-so, or poor? Explain.

(5) Do you agree with the writer's viewpoint? Explain.

GLOSSARY

This glossary is intended to give you a quick idea of the meanings of words as they are used in this textbook. Many of the words have more than one meaning, and you can find these other meanings, of course, by looking up the words in a dictionary.

Words which are explained in the text are not included in this glossary. Examples of such words are "equivalent statements," "converse," and "innuendo." You can locate the definitions of these words by looking in the index to see where the words appear in the text.

adequate (add ih kwuht)—sufficient; enough to get by with.

autopsy (aw tahp see)—detailed medical examination after death in order to determine condition of body and cause of death.

begotten (bih gaht uhn)—produced as offspring.

censor (sen suhr)—a person who sees material to be published and decides whether or not some of it should be changed or eliminated.

centimeter (sent uh meet uhr)—a unit of length equal to about 2/5 of an inch. One inch equals 2.54 centimeters.

certificate (suhr tihf ih kuht)—a document which says it guarantees that something is true.

chauffeur (sho fuhr)—a person who drives a private vehicle for someone.

client (klī uhnt)—a customer of someone in a profession. (When someone hires an attorney, then he is the attorney's client. When he buys groceries, then he is the grocer's customer.)

cm—abbreviation for "centimeter."

consistent (kuhn sis tuhnt)—reasonably uniform in thought or action; not self-contradictory.

degenerate (dih jen uh ruht)—below normal standards, usually in a twisted or otherwise unpleasant way.

deport (dih po(uh)rt)—order and send out of the country.

devastating (dev uh stayt ihng)—(1) extremely attractive. (2) overpoweringly ruinous.

discharge (dis charj)—dismiss or fire from employment.

discipline (dis uh pluhn, or, dis uh plin)—control; training; orderly conduct.

eliminate (ih lim uh nayt)—get rid of; do away with.

elite (ay leet)—well above normal standards; socially superior; of choice quality.

ethnic (eth nihk)—relating to a group having something in common such as customs, nationality, race, or traits.

felony (fel uh nee)—a major crime such as murder or arson or armed robbery.

foster (fos tuhr)—encourage; promote; aid; help develop.

freeloader (free lode uhr)—a person who doesn't pay his own way; someone who gets something for nothing; someone who gets benefits without earning them.

impound (ihm pownd)—confine, as in a prison or a pound; take away and hold by legal authorities.

infest (ihn <u>fest</u>)—be in too much supply; be present in unwelcomingly large numbers.

inflation (ihn <u>flay</u> shuhn)—a condition when a given amount of money will not buy as much (in goods or services) as it used to buy.

integration (ihn tuh <u>gray</u> shuhn)—(1) a mixing together of unlike things, treating them as equals under the circumstances. (If students and teachers eat lunch together, then their lunchroom is <u>integrated</u>. If students of different races attend the same classes in school, then their classes are racially <u>integrated</u>.) (2) a certain process in higher mathematics.

irreconcilable (ihr (r)ek uhn <u>sy</u> luh buhl)—positively unable to reach agreement.

kilogram (<u>kil</u> uh gram)—a unit of weight equal to about 2.2 pounds.

kilometer (<u>kil</u> uh meet uhr, or, kil <u>ahm</u> uht uhr)—a unit of length equal to 1,000 meters or about 3/5 of a mile. One mile is about 1.61 kilometers.

km—abbreviation for "kilometer."

lethal (<u>lee</u> thuhl)—deadly; capable of causing death.

liter (<u>leet</u> uhr)—a unit of liquid measure equal to about 1.1 quarts. One gallon equals about 3.8 liters.

lottery (<u>laht</u> uh ree)—selection of someone (or something) by chance, as, for example, by the drawing of a ticket from a container full of tickets.

manslaughter (<u>man</u> slawt uhr)—the killing of someone through an act of carelessness or negligence. (In manslaughter, there is no intent to do harm; in murder, an intent to do harm is present.)

marijuana (maahr uh <u>wahn</u> uh)—a plant from which cigarettes are made and smoked for their intoxicating effect.

meter (meet uhr)—a unit of length equal to about 39.37 inches. One yard is about .91 of a meter. One meter is about 1.1 yards.

negation (nih <u>gay</u> shuhn)—denial; disagreement; claim that something is untrue.

Orion (uh <u>ry</u> uhn)—a certain group of stars.

perverted (puhr <u>vuhrt</u> uhd)—morally corrupted or twisted.

prosecuting attorney (<u>prahs</u> ih kyewt ihng uh <u>tuhr</u> nee)—a lawyer who presents and argues the government's side of a court case.

racist (<u>ray</u> suhst)—one who believes that people of one race are automatically superior to people of another race.

receptionist (rih <u>sep</u> shuh nuhst)—an employee whose duties include greeting people who come to see someone at a place of business.

refutation (ref yew <u>tay</u> shuhn)—a line of reasoning or argument which refutes another line of reasoning or argument.

refute (rih <u>fyewt</u>)—find fault with or weakness in; tell what's wrong with; find an error in; disprove. (Note: "refute" is applied to reasoning processes, not to people's characters or habits.)

reimburse (ree uhm <u>buhrs</u>)—pay back; repay for expenses. (Example: The traveling salesman paid for his traveling expenses, but his company <u>reimbursed</u> him for them.)

stalemate (<u>stayl</u> mayt)—a position in which it is not possible for either side to gain an advantage or win.

statistic (stuh tihs tik)—a fact in which a number is used. (Examples: "The average American man is 70 inches tall" is a statistic. "Over 25% of the people surveyed said they disliked the product" is a statistic.)

Taj Mahal (tahj maa hahl)—a white marble building in Agra, India renowned for its beauty.

vice versa (vīs vuhr suh, or, vī sih vuhr suh)—the other way around; with the order reversed.

waive (wayv)—forego; give up voluntarily; agree to do without or not to use.

INDEX

Advertising, 119, 122-124, 126, 129
Allegory, 59
"And" sentences, 30-31, 41, 53
   truth value of, 31, 53
Animal breeding, 121
Anticipating arguments, 156, 160-164, 167-169
Antony, Mark, 100 n
Arguing, senseless, 4, 7-10
   stupid, 4, 7-10
Argument, 4-6, 22, 50-52, 55, 135, 157, 160-164, 166-169, 171-172
   anticipating an, 156, 160-164, 167-169
   emotional, 112-113, 140, 150, 172
   good, 140, 149-153, 166-167, 172
     attributes of, 149-151
   refutation of, 161-164, 167-169, 171
Attributes of a good argument, 149-151
Auto buyer, 132
Avoiding the question, 88-89, 93

"Bandwagon," 98-99, 101
"Bargain," 106-107
Beauty and the Beast, 18-19
Brand name, 122, 128-129
Breeding animals, 121

Caesar, Julius, 100 n
Car buyer, 132
"Card-stacking," 114
Career opportunities, 124-125
Certificate, photo, 127
   prize, 127-128
Chain letter, 121
Charities, appeals from, 106-107, 128, 150
Cinderella, 17
Circular reasoning, 86, 93, 149-150
Circumstantial evidence, 72-73
Conclusion, 5, 50-55, 70, 87, 114, 160
   logical, 51-55, 149, 151
Conditions, necessary, 34-36, 48, 54
   sufficient, 34-36, 48, 54
Consecutive, 33
Contest, photo, 127
   puzzle, 127
Contrapositive, 42-46
   truth value of, 43
Converse, 42-44, 46
   substitution of, for proposition, 46, 93
   truth value of, 43

Counterexample, 4, 12-15, 23, 39, 93
   "proof" by failure to find a, 5, 14-15, 23, 93
Courses, job or career, 124-125
Critical thinking, 2-4, 16-17, 22, 39, 57, 59, 64, 70, 72, 81, 110, 114, 157

Debating, 167-169
Definitions, need for, 65-66, 167-168
Disagreement, 4-6, 22
Discount on merchandise, 128
Discussion, 4-6
Display photo, 127
Distributing the undistributed middle term, 91
Double negatives, 32-33
Double standard, 142-144, 154
Drawing a line, 146, 148, 154

Edison, Thomas A., 78
Emotional, arguments, 112-113, 140, 150, 172
   words and phrases, 113, 114, 140-142
Emperor's New Garment, The, 19-20
Equivalent statements, 35, 41, 43, 45, 46, 48
Errors in reasoning (see Faulty reasoning)
Estate, inheritance of, 121
"Everybody does it," 143-146
Evidence, 72-73
"Exigency," 105-107
Eyewitnesses, 72-74

"Factory gate" selling, 128
Fairy tales, 17-22
   Beauty and the Beast, 18-19
   Cinderella, 17
   Emperor's New Garment, The, 19-20
   Princess and the Frog, The, 21-22
   Ugly Duckling, The, 20-21
Faking a connection, 91-93
Faulty reasoning, 85 ff., 114
   (See also Avoiding the question; Circular reasoning; Faking a connection; Propaganda techniques; "Proof" by failure to find a counterexample; "Proof" by selected instances; Special Pleading; Substitution)

Feelings about words, 63-65, 80
Fight, 4-6, 22
"Flag-waving," 115
Flanner, 14, 38
Foreign prisoner, 121
Form of a sentence, 29
"Free," 106, 115

Furnace inspector, 127

Gas and oil wells, 122
General statement, 10-15, 22
"Get rich quick" schemes, 120-122
"Glittering generality," 108-110
Good argument (*see* Argument, good)
Guzzir, 96

Heir, 121
Home, improvement, 128
   inspector, 127
   jobs at, 120-121
   landscaping, 128
   model, 128
   repairs in your neighborhood, 128

"If-then" sentences, 27, 36 *ff.*, 48
   truth value of, 37-39, 54
Implication, 27, 77-78, 82, 103
Inference, 77-78, 103, 105
Inheritance, 121
Innuendo, 110-112
Inspector, 127
Inverse, 42-46
   substitution of, for proposition, 46, 93
   truth value of, 43

Job opportunities, 120-121, 124-125
Job-training courses, 124-125
John, 83
Julius Caesar, 100 *n*
Jury duty, 136-137
"Just plain folks," 115

Kennedy, John F., 70

Landscaping, 128
Law, protection of, 136-137
Letter, chain, 121
Line, drawing a, 146, 148, 154
List price, 128
Literary reference, 59
Logic, 25 *ff.*
Logical conclusion, 51-55, 149, 151

Mark Antony, 100 *n*
Memory, 72-73
Merchandise, unordered, 128
Middle term, distributing the undistributed, 91
Model home, 128
Multiple negatives, 32-33
"Name-calling," 112-113, 115
Name of product or service, 122

Necessary conditions, 34-36, 48, 54
Negation, 33
Negatives, double or multiple, 32-33
Neighborhood, repairs in your, 128
Niemoller, Martin, 152
Norman, George, 79
"Not" signs, 26-27, 33, 41, 53
Nursery stock, 128

Oil and gas wells, 122
Old sayings, 59, 62-63, 80
"Only if" sentences, 47-48
   truth value of, 48
"Or" sentences, 28-29, 41, 53
   truth value of, 29, 53
Oversimplifying, 114

Photo, certificate, 127
   contest, 127
   display, 127
Possible, 58-59, 79
Premise, 50-52, 55, 149-151, 160
   truth value of, 149-150
Princess and the Frog, The, 21-22
Prisoner, foreign, 121
Prize certificate, 127-128
Probable, 58-59, 79
Proof by counterexample (*see* Counter-
   example)
"Proof" by failure to find a counterexample,
   5, 14-15, 23, 93
"Proof" by selected instances, 87, 93
Propaganda techniques, 97 *ff*, 120, 123,
   146
   (*See also* "Bandwagon"; "Bargain"; "Card-
     stacking"; "Exigency"; "Flag-
     waving"; "Free"; "Glittering gen-
     erality"; Innuendo; "Just plain folks";
     Oversimplifying; Repetition; "Snob";
     "Testimonial"; "Transfer")
Proposition, 42-44, 46
Protection of the law, 136-137
Puzzle contest, 127
Pyramid plan, 121

Quotation, from Bible, 83
   from Edison, Thomas A., 78
   from Kennedy, John F., 70
   from Niemoller, Martin, 152
   from Norman, George, 79
   from Twain, Mark, 152

Races, tips on, 121
Reasoning errors (*See* Faulty reasoning)

Recommended selling price, 128
Reference, literary, 59
Refutation of argument, 161-164, 167-169, 171
Repairs in your neighborhood, 128
Repetition, 98, 100-101
Rules of society, 136
Ruses (*see* Schemes)

Schemes, 119-122, 124 125, 127-129, 132
Selling price, 128
Senseless arguing, 4, 7-10
Sentence, form of, 29
Shakespeare, 100 *n*
"Snob," 115
Society, rules of, 136, 153
 laws in, 136-137
Spare-time earnings, 120
Special pleading, 90, 93, 136, 142
Standard, double, 142-144, 154
Statement, general, 10-15, 22
Stupid, advertisements, 126
 arguing, 4, 7-10
Substitution, of converse for proposition, 46, 93
 of inverse for proposition, 46, 93
Sufficient conditions, 34-36, 48, 54
Swindles (*see* Schemes)
Symbols, 26-28, 53

Tattoos, 29-31, 38, 45, 53, 81
Termite inspector, 128
"Testimonial," 103-104, 115
Thinking, critical, 2-4, 16-17, 22, 39, 57, 59, 64, 70, 72, 81, 110, 114, 157
Tips on races, 121
"Transfer," 92, 101-102, 115
Tricks of memory, 72-73
Truth table, 38, 41-42
Truth value, of "and" sentence, 31, 53
 of contrapositive, 43
 of converse, 43
 of "if-then" sentence, 37-39, 54
 of inverse, 43
 of "only if" sentence, 48
 of "or" sentence, 29, 53
 of premise, 149-150
Twain, Mark, 152

Ugly Duckling, The, 20-21
Unordered merchandise, 128
Used car, 132

Value judgments, 135, 146-149, 153

Wells, gas and oil, 122
Where the line is drawn, 146, 148, 154

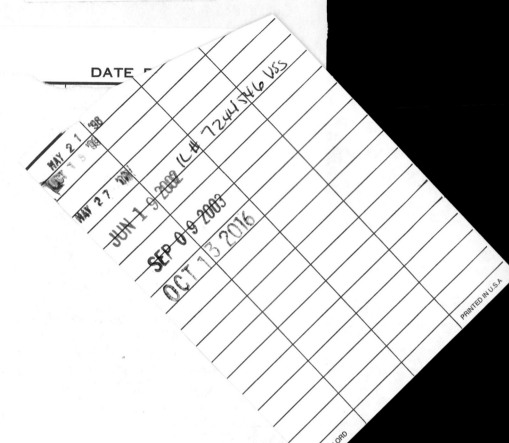